NORTH CAROLINA

STRING MUSIC MASTERS

OLD-TIME AND BLUEGRASS LEGENDS

Elizabeth A. Carlson

Foreword by Former NPR Journalist Paul Brown

THE
History
PRESS

Published by The History Press
Charleston, SC
www.historypress.net

Front cover, bottom: David Holt, Grandfather Mountain, North Carolina, 2002.
Photo by Hugh Morton, courtesy of David Holt.

First published 2016

Manufactured in the United States

ISBN 978.1.60949.853.5

Library of Congress Control Number: 2015954758

I dedicate this book to my husband and daughters
for their encouragement and love
and to the memory of my parents and grandparents,
who shared with me their passion for American music.

CONTENTS

FOREWORD

This is a book of life stories. Here you will encounter remarkable people whose paths intertwine not so much in time as in qualities, place, music and love.

Elizabeth Carlson could have written about hundreds of North Carolina musicians and still been far from finished. So she made careful choices, thinking about what binds southern—and specifically North Carolina—musicians and music traditions together. She picked seven people who embody the deep creativity and cultural encounters important to the evolution of the state's music traditions.

You'll find numerous common threads in the stories of these seven people. Among them:

Paul Brown at the newscast mic, NPR, Washington, D.C., circa 2004. *Courtesy of the Collection of Paul Brown.*

- Abundant curiosity about music all around, near and far.
- A fascination with musical elders and what they can show us about how to play and how to be.

- The commitment to be observant, to listen and then to create music with new energy, for new generations, from what has come before.
- Belief in the value of the gift of life.
- The illuminating power of hardship in creating great music and positive changes in one's life.

Dive in and swim along in the current of Elizabeth Carlson's natural, welcoming storytelling. You will come to understand North Carolina as you might never have before. You will also discover wonderful aspects of what it is to be a musician through the stories of these intense, unusual yet universal North Carolina characters.

PAUL BROWN
Musician, producer, former NPR journalist
Winston-Salem, March 2015

PREFACE

If I am obsessed with what American music tells us about our past, it comes from my father, Andrew Anspach. Dad grew up in the 1920s and '30s in a suburb twenty miles from New York City and played the saxophone and clarinet. After college, combat in World War II and law school, Dad wanted to hear jazz in smoky nightclubs rather than shuffle papers in stuffy law firms.

Through a grand stroke of luck, he got the chance to run the historic Algonquin Hotel in Manhattan from 1957 to 1987. The hotel was a dining spot and home-away-from-home for celebrities in the arts and letters. It was also beloved by Broadway theatergoers from all walks of life.

Dad started a cabaret and supper club in the Oak Room at the hotel, just blocks away from the theaters where many Algonquin guests attended and performed. The Oak Room at the Algonquin became one of the country's leading cabarets, helping launch the careers of musicians such as Michael Feinstein, Harry Connick Jr. and Diana Krall.

I loved going there, and to other great music spots around the city, with Dad. We'd catch a bus to Lincoln Center to hear Leonard Bernstein's Young People's Concerts. We'd cram into a cab with my mom and sister and head downtown to enjoy a Broadway musical. We'd rush off to the Cookery in Greenwich Village to catch blues legend Alberta Hunter.

One of Dad's interesting friends in New York, a concert pianist, told him about an artsy camp in Vermont she'd found for her three sons. Dad decided this was the camp for me. Little did he know that sending me there would spark my love for old-time and bluegrass music.

The author's father with his granddaughters, New York City, 1997. *Photo by the author.*

In 1971, off I went to Camp Killooleet in Hancock, Vermont. John Seeger, a gifted educator who was also Pete Seeger's brother, ran the camp with his wife, Ellie. The other campers and I had the time of our lives sitting around the campfire listening to our counselors play songs on their guitars and banjos. We sang our hearts out as we tapped our feet on our toasty blankets near the crackling fire. To my ears, even better sounding than the music I'd heard back home with Dad was this rural music, which sounded both exotic and familiar.

Decades later, in 1995, after living in Washington, D.C.; San Francisco; and Boston, I moved with my husband and young daughters to North Carolina. A bluegrass song on the radio led to an old-time jam at a coffeehouse, which led to a bluegrass festival, and pretty soon I realized that by good fortune I had landed in the mother lode of old-time and bluegrass music. But, thanks to Hollywood and the mass media, this music still brought to my mind the clichéd image of white geezers in overalls picking banjos on the front porch.

Then one day, while listening to a local public radio show in Winston-Salem, I heard the show's learned host, Paul Brown, talk about the African American influences in old-time and bluegrass music. My interest was piqued.

I contacted Paul, and we met for coffee in downtown Winston-Salem. Paul was delightful and knew everything about old-time and bluegrass music. He'd grown up in a New York City suburb and had played the banjo since age ten. By chance, his mother, a book editor of southern extraction, had often lunched with publishing colleagues at the Algonquin Hotel.

I loved this guy. With his help, I contacted a dozen musicians in Winston-Salem and formed a nonprofit group, Carolina Music Ways. I still work for the group, researching the diverse musical heritage of North Carolina and creating assembly shows and related curricula for schools. The website of Carolina Music Ways caught the eye of an editor at The History Press and led to this book.

In writing the book, I've had the chance to learn about some amazing people. The musicians profiled are not only musical trailblazers but also human beings who have triumphed over hardship. Their stories speak to the power of the human spirit and the power of music. These musical pioneers have inspired me deeply, and I hope they do the same for you.

One book cannot possibly cover all the great North Carolina old-time and bluegrass musicians. In deciding whom to include, I chose musicians who had interesting stories. I also looked for variety to make the book more interesting to write, as well as to read.

Of the musicians profiled in this book, the one who clearly falls in the bluegrass camp is Earl Scruggs. He helped create the original bluegrass sound. Charlie Poole was a forefather of bluegrass. Doc Watson played a mix of styles, including a lot of old-time and some bluegrass. Tommy Jarrell and Joe Thompson were old-time musicians. David Holt and Rhiannon Giddens—the two musicians alive today—play an eclectic mix. Much of what they play is old-time with a new twist.

I hope you enjoy learning more about these awesome musicians and, in the process, more about North Carolina, the mecca of bluegrass and old-time music I happily call home.

I adored Dad and think of him every day. Dad loved music's unifying power. Doc Watson viewed music as "a bridge between different peoples and cultures," and Dad saw music in a similar way. Dad—like Watson and all the musicians profiled in this book—understood that music connects people, broadens their worlds and heals their spirits.

ACKNOWLEDGEMENTS

One of the most enjoyable aspects of this project was conducting lengthy, in-person interviews. I am grateful to Dr. Foster Hirsch, film historian at Brooklyn College, for sharing with me his terrific interviewing techniques.

I give my heartfelt gratitude to the many people I interviewed for this book who shared their wonderful stories, research and insights.

For the Charlie Poole chapter, thanks to Kinney Rorrer, Charlie Poole's grandnephew and biographer; Gail Knauff, director of the Haw River Historical Museum; and L. McKay "Mac" Whatley, president of the Randolph Heritage Conservancy.

For the Tommy Jarrell chapter, thanks to Paul Brown, old-time musician and former NPR journalist, and Alan Jabbour, founding director of the American Folklife Center at the Library of Congress.

For the Joe Thompson chapter, thanks to Dr. Iris Thompson Chapman, Joe's second cousin and documentarian; Bob Carlin, banjo musician and historian; Dr. Kip Lornell, ethnomusicologist at George Washington University; and Dellaphine Ivey, Joe's niece.

David Watson, Doc's brother, was very helpful with the Doc Watson chapter, as were Doc's nephew Kermit Watson, Ginny and David Holt and Angie Greene, who graciously hosted the interview session.

For the Earl Scruggs chapter, thanks to Jim Mills, bluegrass musician and historian and friend of the legendary Earl Scruggs. One of the great pleasures in writing this book was interviewing Jim Mills in his showroom filled with vintage bluegrass memorabilia and prewar Gibson banjos.

For the chapter on David Holt, thanks to David Holt himself, who went above and beyond in helping and encouraging me throughout this project.

For the chapter on Rhiannon Giddens, thanks to Rhiannon Giddens herself, who took time from her international touring schedule to grant me a wide-ranging, two-hour interview. Thanks also to Dom Flemons, a founding member of the Carolina Chocolate Drops, for his information about the group and African American music history.

I took great care in editing this book. Thanks to the wonderful people who assisted me: Eric Carlson for line edits, Bob Carlin for music history edits and Andrew Szanton for style suggestions. Thanks also to Jaime Muehl, senior production editor at The History Press, for her excellent copyedits and to Banks Smither, my commissioning editor at The History Press, for his superb overall guidance.

An enormous amount of research went into this book. The Z. Smith Reynolds Library at Wake Forest University is a great research library, with an outstanding collection of books on music. Thanks to the library's fine staff, especially to Mary Reeves, reserves and media coordinator. Thanks also to Stephen Culkin, resource librarian at the Greensboro Public Library, and to old-time musician Fred Mock, who loaned me a number of books from his own library.

For helping me locate and secure rights to the photos in this book, thanks to the staff at the Wilson Library at the University of North Carolina at Chapel Hill, most notably Aaron Smithers at the Southern Folklife Collection and Keith Longiotti at the North Carolina Collection. Thanks also to Eric Blevins and Kent Thompson at the North Carolina Museum of History and to William Brown at the State Archives of North Carolina. For helping me with the MerleFest photos, thanks to Amber Herman and Bethany Swaim at Wilkes Community College and to Lauren May with Andy May's Acoustic Kids. Thanks also to the many photographers who granted me permission to use their wonderful photos in this book.

I'd also like to thank the artists who created delightful art for the book: Ann Elkington for her lovely North Carolina map and Tracy Bigelow Grisman for her charming drawings.

Finally, I'd like to thank my cousins Douglas and Michael for their encouragement and insights and my wonderful husband and daughters for their valued feedback and unwavering support.

I worked diligently, in the writing of this book, to be as thorough as I could and to use sources that were reliable and consistent with other sources. For any inaccuracies in this book, I apologize. Though each of the people I've acknowledged here has been very helpful to me, all of the mistakes in the book are mine.

WHAT'S THE DIFFERENCE BETWEEN OLD-TIME AND BLUEGRASS?

"Fiddle and Banjo." *Drawing by Tracy Bigelow Grisman, 2015.*

To get the most out of this book, it's useful to understand what "old-time" music is and where it comes from and what "bluegrass" is and where that comes from.

First, let me try to explain "old-time" music.

"Mountain" music, "Appalachian" music, "string band" music, "traditional" music, "hillbilly" music and "old-time" music—they're all different terms for basically the same thing.

I like the term "old-time" best.

"The Old Barn Floor," published by Currier & Ives, circa 1868, New York. *Courtesy of the Library of Congress, Prints & Photographs Division.*

For centuries, this kind of music has been played all across North Carolina, so I don't use the term "mountain" or "Appalachian" music. "String band" sounds like a bunch of musicians, but sometimes this music is played by as few as two. "Traditional" sounds like something folklorists would say. I won't call it "hillbilly" because that brings to mind two old guys with corncob pipes.

That leaves "old-time." Short. Easy to remember. Folksy but not corny.

Old-time music, like everything else American, is a fascinating mix.

When the banjo came to this country with African slaves, there was the strange idea that black people and white people were supposed to stay apart. But the music resisted. The banjo needed the fiddle brought by the colonists, and the fiddle needed the banjo. Anyone who played the music knew it was twice as rich when the two instruments were played together.

When the banjo and fiddle mixed, a new American style of music was born: old-time. Later, other stringed instruments—like the guitar—joined in.

What black and white musicians created in the South was a delicious, rich gumbo called old-time—fiddle tunes from the British Isles here, banjo breakdowns there, minstrel songs for flavor, Victorian parlor songs for texture and Tin Pan Alley favorites for flair. Gospel hymns and bluesy numbers gave the mix added zing.

Many people throughout North Carolina played old-time music. Families proudly passed down their instruments and songs from one generation to the next. Folks enjoyed old-time music with neighbors and friends on farms and in small towns.

At its core, old-time was dance music. In the days before radio, old-time was the music of country folk, both blacks and whites. People danced joyously to the sounds of the fiddle and banjo after a hard day's work on the farm. Folks were thrilled to get together and dance for hours in barns and homes. It was a way for young people to flirt with and court one another. Folks of all ages held hands and joined hearts as they moved around in squares to the lively beats.

Bluegrass, on the other hand, is show music. It doesn't come from the community; it's presented to the community, mostly on a stage. People don't dance to bluegrass; they listen to it.

Bluegrass was born in the early 1940s, though it wasn't called by that name for about a decade. Many of the pioneers of bluegrass were southerners with rural roots working in mill towns. They mixed the old-time music they were raised on with pop sounds of the day that they heard on records and radio. These included big band and swing, gospel quartet and blues.

A typical bluegrass band has a three-finger banjo picker, a fiddler, a guitarist, a mandolin player and an upright bass player. The band members take exciting solo breaks, as in jazz. Vocals are more important in bluegrass than in old-time, with stirring harmonies often taking center stage.

A classic bluegrass band is known for its intense, rapid-fire music. Alan Lomax, a famous folklorist, referred to bluegrass as "folk music in overdrive."

Bluegrass and old-time music are both terrific. So are the seven musicians you're about to meet. Let's get started.

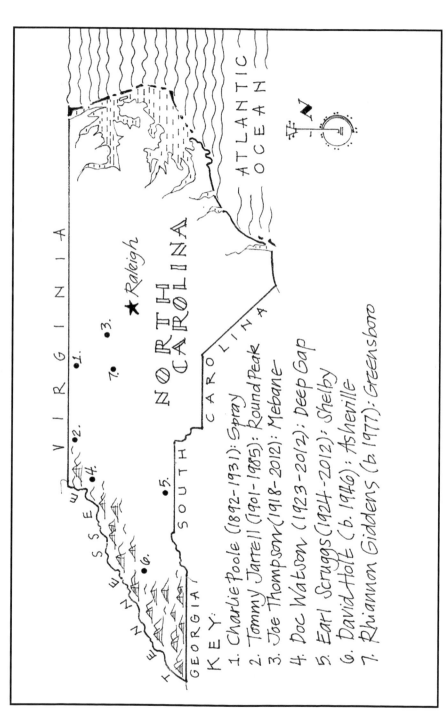

KEY:
1. Charlie Poole (1892-1931): Spray
2. Tommy Jarrell (1901-1985): Round Peak
3. Joe Thompson (1918-2012): Mebane
4. Doc Watson (1923-2012): Deep Gap
5. Earl Scruggs (1924-2012): Shelby
6. David Holt (b. 1946): Asheville
7. Rhiannon Giddens (b. 1977): Greensboro

Map by Ann Elkington, 2015.

CHARLIE POOLE

VISION

At-a-Glance

DATES: *1892–1931*
INSTRUMENTS: *Banjo, vocals*
MUSIC STYLES: *Old-time*
HOME: *Millboro, Haw River, Greensboro, and Spray, North Carolina*
LEGACY: *Poole was one of the first and greatest old-time music recording stars. His three-finger banjo picking contained the blueprint for bluegrass, the style of music he helped bring about but did not live to see. He is sometimes called "the grandfather of bluegrass."*

THE POOLES OF RANDOLPH COUNTY

Charles Cleveland Poole was born in 1892 and spent his first ten years in Randolph County, North Carolina. His father, John Phillip Poole, was a textile millworker. Like many of his peers, he had fled the hardships of life on the farm in search of a steady paycheck. Charlie Poole's mother, Bettie Ellen Johnson Poole, was also from country stock. She worked at home—cooking, tending the garden and taking care of her eight children.

The Poole family rented a house in Millboro, a rural area of Randolph County that was a station stop on the Cape Fear and Yadkin Valley

Charlie Poole, Spray, North Carolina, 1925. *Courtesy of the Kinney Rorrer Collection.*

Railroad. Millboro was the shipping point in the county where mill agents sent off textile products and picked up cotton. It was also home to many moonshiners. Apple brandy was a local specialty.

Living in Millboro, Charlie's father was within walking distance of three villages and their mills: Worthville, Franklinville and Cedar Falls. At one point or another, Mr. Poole probably worked in all three. Charlie's older sister, Sarah, and his two older brothers, Leroy and Ralph, also worked in the mills.

THE BREADTH OF RANDOLPH COUNTY MUSIC

Growing up in the 1890s, Charlie Poole heard loads of live music. Charlie was surrounded by many relatives and family friends who played old-time music. On front porches, in backyards and at house parties, Charlie heard the lively sounds of fiddles and banjos.

Throughout the year, folks gathered at tent revival meetings for spirited shape note singing. Likely, Charlie went to these revivals and probably also to traveling tent shows featuring minstrel acts.

Most minstrel acts featured whites in blackface playing clawhammer banjo, an African-derived style with a down-stroking motion that strummed all the strings at once. Clawhammer banjo was associated with blacks because slaves brought the banjo from Africa and played in this style. Over time, slaves taught European Americans how to play.

When whites adopted the instrument, professional musicians played it in rough circuses and minstrel shows. One of the first whites known to play the banjo in the North Carolina Piedmont was Manly Reese (1830–1864) from Randolph County. Reese may have learned to play the banjo from a slave or from someone else who learned from a slave. Reese played many Stephen Foster songs and may have learned them from traveling minstrel shows.

In the 1890s, when Charlie Poole was growing up in the North Carolina Piedmont, the banjo was a popular instrument that both blacks and whites liked to play. By the time he was seven years old, Charlie could play the banjo, shown how by his father and older brother Leroy. Charlie loved the banjo so much that he made himself one out of a large gourd, similar to the ones slaves had made decades earlier.

"CLASSIC" BANJO CRAZE

When Charlie was a boy—fifty years after Manly Reese learned to play clawhammer banjo—another style was growing in popularity around the nation: the "classic" finger-picking style, derived from classical guitar. In "classic" banjo, instead of the clawhammer's down-strumming motion, three fingers "up-picked" the strings.

The banjo rose from its humble roots as the classic banjo craze swept the country. Through records and touring vaudeville shows, the banjo became part of national pop culture. People viewed it as a "respectable" middle-class instrument, suitable for college banjo clubs, fancy parlors and concert stages. Now the banjo brought to mind tuxedos and top hats.

The three-finger technique used by the classic banjoists made it possible to play more complex melodies. The most popular classic banjoists were northern, middle-class musicians Vess Ossman (1868–1923) and Fred Van Eps (1878–1960). Their records were national hits. Ossman's and Van Eps's three-finger picking technique suited a range of songs, including ragtime, classical works and songs from Tin Pan Alley, the street in New York City where songwriters churned out many of the day's popular tunes.

In the 1890s, the classic banjo craze affected much, though not all, of North Carolina. Most banjo players in the North Carolina mountains still played the clawhammer style. But in the Piedmont, where Charlie lived, most banjoists were now playing the new, classic three-finger style. One of them was the young Charlie Poole.

POOLE'S TALENTED COUSIN DANER JOHNSON

When Charlie was growing up in Millboro, the best classic three-finger style banjoist from the North Carolina Piedmont was a sporadic millworker and wandering musician from Randolph County named Daner Johnson (1879–1955).

Johnson was a hugely talented and sophisticated banjo player. He preferred the classic three-finger style and was a master of it. Likely, he had learned the style from listening to phonograph records and watching musicians in touring vaudeville and medicine shows. According to family members, in 1904, Johnson won first place in a banjo contest in St. Louis, beating out the famous Fred Van Eps. It was even rumored that Johnson had played his banjo in such faraway places as England and California and at Gloria Vanderbilt's high-society wedding in New York.

This remarkable musician, thirteen years older than Charlie, was his second cousin on his mother's side. He taught Charlie's older brother Leroy how to play. Since they were closely related and lived within a few miles of each other, Charlie likely saw Daner fairly often. How much did Daner Johnson influence Charlie Poole? According to banjo historian Bob Carlin, a great deal.

MILLWORKER CHILDHOOD IN HAW RIVER

Shortly after 1900, when Charlie was almost eight years old, he moved with his family to Haw River, a mill village in neighboring Alamance County. The county was home to one of the largest clusters of mills in the state. Charlie's father and older siblings went to work in the mills.

Haw River was a typical mill town. A few miles east of Burlington, it was on a river and a railroad line. The town bustled with two thousand residents and had the feel of a big family. The center of life was the mills: the Granite Cotton Mill and the Cora Mill across the street.

Millworkers such as the Pooles worked long hours for little pay. A typical workweek ran from 6:00 a.m. to 6:00 p.m., Monday through Friday, with a half day on Saturday. The pay was about three dollars a week. The mills were hot, loud, dusty and dangerous. There were no child labor laws, and the mills were filled with child workers.

Even though Charlie was school age when he arrived in Haw River, he never attended school there. School attendance was not required in North Carolina until 1913. Until his thirties, Charlie Poole was illiterate. He was also very smart and verbally gifted—a frustrating mix.

Before Charlie entered full-time millwork, he played with the other children when his chores were done. Large groups of kids roamed the town and nearby countryside, playing ball games, swinging from trees and swimming in the river. They picked blackberries and peaches in the summer and slid down slippery slopes in the winter.

Charlie also spent as much time as he could picking his homemade gourd banjo.

When he was around nine, Charlie began full-time millwork. He began as a doffer, a typical job for boys. Doffers worked about half of every hour, giving them free time to play. But when doffers worked, it was at breakneck speed. When the bobbins were filled with yarn, doffers snatched them and replaced them with empty ones. Sometimes, doffers needed to climb on the machinery, and they could slip and get caught in the bobbins and spindles. Charlie managed to avoid any serious accidents, but the work was nerve-wracking.

HAW RIVER'S MUSIC

Aside from baseball, the main source of amusement in Haw River was music, and it was everywhere. Every free moment, musicians of all ages played their banjos and fiddles. Every day of the week, music jams crowded front porches, and on Saturday nights, there were lively house parties. Townspeople would pick a house, clear out the furniture and dance until the wee hours of the morning.

There were other occasions for music, too. Music was front and center at holiday parties, celebrations and christenings. People sang at community sing-alongs, church and tent revivals. Music came through town with traveling shows.

Charlie heard all kinds of instruments. Residents of Scots-Irish extraction played fiddles and bagpipes. People of German descent played accordions and zithers. Townspeople of African American lineage played ocarinas and banjos.

Charlie also likely listened to records. He may have heard them in the homes of the town's wealthier residents during community open houses or on visits to friends. Charlie would also have likely heard records played on a coin-operated machine at the general store.

In this music-rich setting, Charlie kept improving his banjo playing. Working full time, he earned enough money to give up his homemade gourd banjo and buy himself a real one for $1.50. Other musicians worked at the mill, and during lull times and on breaks, Charlie played music with them and shared playing techniques. Before long, Charlie Poole was known as one of the area's best banjoists.

ROWDY TEENAGER

As a teenager, Charlie occupied his time with other pastimes, too. Haw River, like any Piedmont mill town, had its share of drinkers and fighters. Charlie was one of the wilder ones; he was arrested a number of times for public drunkenness.

One day, Charlie, an avid baseball player, made a bet with another youth that he could catch a ball without a glove no matter how fast and hard it was thrown at him. He closed his hand too soon. The ball slammed into his fingers, and several of them broke. They didn't heal properly and became permanently curled over in an arch, with the fingertips pointing to the center of his palm.

Years later, when an admirer asked him how he could learn to play the banjo like he did, Charlie answered that he should break his fingers first.

Another time, when he was drunk, Charlie and some of his brothers hijacked the newly built streetcar running from Haw River to Burlington. They threw off the passengers and conductor and then drove the car on a short joy ride. Charlie and his brothers got in some trouble for that.

Incidents like this earned Charlie the reputation among police as a practical joker with a wild streak. But despite his rowdy image, many policemen liked him and were keen on his music. Sometimes, instead of arresting him, they'd invite him to their homes to play his banjo for a dance.

THE BEST MUSICIAN IN THE MILL

By 1912, Charlie Poole was nineteen with both his parents dead. Soon, he found someone who tried to tame him. That year, he married seventeen-year-old Maude Gibson, a millworker from Haw River. Charlie and Maude moved in with her parents.

Maude hoped that Charlie would mend his rowdy ways, but he continued to drink. He skipped work to play his banjo on the streets of town. Clearly, his top priority was not bringing money home to his wife.

Some days, he played very close to the mill, on the bridge over the river. Millworkers, leading very hard lives, heard his music and hung their heads out of windows. The mill managers fired Charlie for missing work. But when they realized that workers were leaving their stations to listen to him play, they rehired him.

Charlie Poole, Spray, North Carolina, 1925. *Courtesy of the Kinney Rorrer Collection.*

In 1913, Charlie, Maude and their infant son, James, moved thirty miles to Greensboro. There, Charlie took a job in the spinning room at the Pomona Cotton Mill. When taking breaks, he played songs like "Can I Sleep in Your Barn Tonight Mister," a tune that he would turn into a hit record over a decade later.

MARRIED RAMBLER

For the next six years, from ages twenty to twenty-six, Charlie Poole played music not only at work but also on the road. He loved to ramble the countryside with his banjo and would leave his job to do it. Before long, he was away for weeks at a time, not letting Maude or anyone else know where he was or when he'd return.

He craved the open road, discovering new places and meeting new people. He'd hop on a railroad car, walk long distances or hitch a ride. He played at farmhouses, in mill towns and at mining camps. He traveled around North Carolina, Virginia and West Virginia and farther still to Tennessee, Kentucky and even 1,500 miles west to Montana.

He busked in front of general stores and on courthouse squares, putting out a cap for change. He played at house parties, square dances and corn shuckings. Often, people who enjoyed his music would offer him a place to stay, home-cooked meals and ample liquor. A few days later, he would move on. On some of these trips, he traveled alone; on others, he'd take along one or two musician friends.

Listeners were drawn to Charlie's charming, witty nature. Along his routes, he joked with folks he met, especially children and seniors. Kinney Rorrer, Charlie's great-nephew and biographer, has written wonderfully about how Charlie used to go into towns and greet people with rhymes like "Hey, Russell, want to tussle?" He called all the women he met "daughter." When Charlie Poole entered a town, fun followed.

UNIQUE MUSIC ATTRACTS CROWDS

Charlie had a one-of-a-kind personality, but what really drew people to him was his music. Everywhere he played, listeners ate up his performance and left wanting more.

People loved Charlie's unique voice. He sang like he talked. His voice was southern and rural but also crisp and sharp. It stood head and shoulders above the typical musician busking for change.

People also enjoyed his fine three-finger banjo picking, which allowed him to play a variety of songs. He played folk songs from the Piedmont and mountain regions that had been passed down through the generations. He also played popular Tin Pan Alley songs from the late nineteenth century and of the day. These included songs made famous by Charlie's favorite, Al Jolson. Charlie played ragtime numbers, too, as well as tunes made famous by classic style banjoists Vess Ossman and Fred Van Eps.

Charlie played in a very similar style to Van Eps, Ossman and Daner Johnson. Fred Van Eps was the musician Charlie admired most and tried to copy. But Charlie did not know all the noting, did not read music and did not play straight classical pieces as Van Eps did. Charlie did a more rural version of classic banjo. And no one did it better than Charlie Poole.

TOO MUCH FOR MAUDE

Charlie's musical wanderings—though a source of joy for many—were a source of frustration for Maude. Ten months after they were married, Charlie was on one of his musical ramblings when their only child, James, was born. Charlie was farther away than usual—in Canada.

By 1917, Charlie was nearing the end of the line with Maude. The family was living in Jamestown, near Greensboro, and Charlie was working in a mill. Maude convinced Charlie to move to a better-paying mill job in Danville, Virginia. He missed meeting her, James and his in-laws at the Greensboro train station because he was in jail for public drunkenness. It was the last straw. Charlie and Maude divorced.

Years later, in discussing her ex-husband, Maude exclaimed, "Ramble! He couldn't be still! He loved to go. You couldn't have a conversation with him. He was gone! But he never stayed over a month in any town [he visited] in his life."

PARTNERSHIP WITH POSEY RORER

In the winter of 1918, shortly after his divorce and during one of his rambles, the twenty-six-year-old Charlie Poole was playing music in the coalfields of West Virginia. In a mining camp there, Charlie met a club-footed fiddler about his age named Posey Rorer (1891–1936).* Their first meeting was likely in Big Stick, West Virginia, at a miners' dance.

---

* Posey was an uncle of Poole biographer Kinney Rorer, but his name was spelled differently.

Posey Rorer was an excellent fiddler from Franklin County, Virginia, about ninety miles southeast of Big Stick. He had left the small family farm where he grew up—a two-room cabin on thirty-eight hilly acres—to earn a paycheck in the mines. Posey had a low-paying job. His two club feet kept him from going deep into the mines. To supplement his small salary, he played his fiddle at house parties and dances.

Charlie and Posey hit it off as friends, drinking buddies and musical partners. Before long, they formed a banjo and fiddle duo. Posey's playing style matched up well with Charlie's. Posey had been playing the fiddle since childhood. He knew many songs passed down in families in the Blue Ridge Mountains.

In the fall of 1918, a worldwide emergency—the Spanish flu epidemic—caused Posey and Charlie to leave the coalfields. Posey's parents and siblings had fallen gravely ill. Posey, with his new friend in tow, rushed back to Franklin County. The two men nursed the frail Rorer clan back to health with hot coffee laced with whiskey.

Charlie moved in with the brood. He and Posey entertained local farmers for small change as they pondered how to make more money. When Homer Philpott, a big local moonshiner, offered Charlie and Posey the chance to join him in a business venture, they jumped at it.

Prohibition had been in effect in Virginia since 1914, but liquor was flowing in Franklin County. It was easier to get liquor than water. When Prohibition took hold across the nation six years later, the "wettest" place in the country would not be New York City or Chicago but Franklin County, Virginia.

Tending their still in the woods, the men made two hundred gallons of liquor a day. Waiting for hours for the liquor to condense, Charlie and Posey killed time playing songs such as "Don't Let Your Brew Go Down," a parody of "Don't Let Your Deal Go Down Blues." Charlie had learned the original from Leaksville musician Tyler Meeks, who, in 1911, had learned it from Charlie Blackstock, an African American musician. Charlie and Posey, sitting by their secret still in the backwoods, never dreamed that seven years later, their recording of this tune would be a huge hit.

From their moonshining scheme, Charlie and Posey each netted the staggering sum of $1,100. Posey set aside the money for an operation at John Hopkins University Hospital in Baltimore to correct his deformed feet. Charlie spent $132 on an Orpheum No. 3 banjo.

SPRAY AND LOU EMMA

The Rorers were barely able to eke out a living from farming their hillside. Around 1919, shortly after Charlie and Posey's moonshining gig ended, the Rorer clan decided to move down the mountains to work in the cotton mills in Spray, North Carolina. Millwork offered them a steadier income. After selling their farm, the Rorers headed fifty miles south to Spray, aided by a family friend driving their possessions on his truck. Charlie offered to bring the family cow on foot. He arrived in Spray three days later with an exhausted cow.

Spray was in Rockingham County, where Eden, North Carolina, is today, ten miles from the Virginia line. Charlie's older sister, Sarah Poole Weaver, lived and worked there, as did Posey's older sister, Lou Emma. They were two of the few thousand millworkers living in the adjacent mill villages of Spray, Leaksville and Draper.

Charlie, now twenty-eight, landed a job at the Leaksville Cotton Mill. Posey and his father found work at the Nantucket Mill. It's likely that, at first, Charlie lived with his sister Sarah and her family.

Charlie began courting Posey's sister Lou Emma, almost ten years his senior. On December 11, 1920, Charlie and Lou Emma married. They moved into Lou Emma's house on Flynn Street. Smart, literate and strong, Lou Emma was devoted to her husband, despite his drinking and rambling. She was wild about the charming and handsome Charlie Poole.

SPRAY'S VIBRANT MUSIC SCENE

The town's musicians also embraced Charlie. He added something new to Spray's already strong old-time music scene—fine banjo playing combined with a unique singing voice. Fiddlers and guitarists were in ample supply in Spray, but there were few banjoists. Rarer still were ones who sang.

It was a golden time and setting for music. Many of the millworkers had come from the North Carolina and Virginia mountains and had brought with them their rich music traditions. Many fine old-time musicians also lived across the Virginia line from Spray, in the textile towns of Fieldale and Danville. Musicians from all the towns shared techniques and songs. In the 1920s, the Spray-Fieldale-Danville area was one of the nation's strongest old-time music centers.

Mill owners also loved music and launched first-rate community music programs. They imported classically trained teachers from Europe. Norwegian

Paul Manker ran the free music programs in the schools. He conducted brass bands, a chorus and junior and symphony orchestras. He also taught group classes and private lessons in guitar, violin and mandolin.

The mill owners also imported another top-notch music teacher: Otto Kircheis from Germany. Kircheis, like Manker, valued the local old-time talent and didn't look down on what some local elites viewed as lower-class music. In fact, Kircheis became a champion of the area's vibrant fiddlers' contests, often serving as a judge. Once, he awarded Charlie Poole first place.

POOLE FORMS A TRIO

Charlie loved playing with Posey Rorer and guitarist William Woodlieff. Before long, they formed a trio. Often, the group played in front of the Spray post office on Saturday afternoons, attracting millworkers and farmers shopping in nearby stores. The three also performed at area house parties, square dances and school graduations. William Woodlieff's younger brother Norman had recently returned from the navy, and when William got married, Norman replaced him in the trio.

Besides playing locally, Charlie, Posey and Norman would leave their mill jobs and ramble through the Virginia and West Virginia mountains. The three hoboed on the rails, hitched rides and walked long distances. They played at general stores and dances, busked for small change and won many fiddlers' contests.

Folks in farm towns and coal camps warmly welcomed the trio. The group stayed in cheap lodgings or with local families. When they stayed with families, Charlie was popular with the very young and old, humoring them with stories. Norman was an excellent artist who often sketched his host's portrait. What the hosts loved most of all was listening to the trio's awesome music. When the musicians left to return to millwork in Spray, their hosts were sad to say goodbye.

THE NORTH CAROLINA RAMBLERS

Around 1924, inspired by the trio's acclaim in Spray and on the road, Charlie decided to name the group the North Carolina Ramblers.

In 1925, they hit the road for a tour through North Carolina textile villages, Virginia mountain farms, West Virginia coal camps and southeastern Ohio towns. The group played at community dances, house parties and fiddlers' conventions. Norman acted as the advance man, going ahead of Charlie and Posey to pass out handbills for shows. In the evenings, the North Carolina Ramblers played to sold-out audiences in roadhouses and school auditoriums.

In the spring of 1925, their tour ended when a promoter they'd met on the road scammed the trio. Demoralized and out of money, they returned to the mills.

One evening, Charlie and Posey went to Leaksville Junction, North Carolina, near the Virginia line, to play at a dance for bootlegger friends. Lawmen raided the party. On the verge of being arrested, Charlie crashed his banjo over a policeman's head. A fight broke out, and another policeman put a gun in Charlie's ear. As the officer pulled the trigger, Charlie pushed down on the barrel. The bullet went off near Charlie's mouth, chipping his teeth and bloodying his lips.

When Charlie went on trial in Spray, the judge asked if he needed a lawyer. With his typical wit, he answered, "No, Your Honor, but I need some good witnesses!" It took Lou Emma a great many hours in the mill to pay the $100 fine that the judge slapped on Charlie Poole.

DETERMINED TO CUT A RECORD

By the spring of 1925, Charlie had recovered from his legal ordeal and decided to follow his dream to cut a record. Two years earlier, the first southern fiddle record had hit the market. It was by Fiddlin' John Carson from Georgia on the Okeh Records label. In 1924, Ernest "Pop" Stoneman—a musician from Virginia who had accompanied the North Carolina Ramblers on their recent tour—had also cut two songs for Okeh. Other southern old-time musicians were also making records, which the record companies were marketing as "hillbilly" music. Charlie felt sure his songs would sell. He knew that the North Carolina Ramblers already had a following among southern farmers and factory workers.

Early one morning in May 1925, Charlie, Posey and Norman went to the mill to collect their paychecks. They sat down at the end of one of the rows of looms. As they played "Don't Let Your Deal Go Down Blues," workers gathered around. When the song stopped, the trio announced that they were quitting their factory jobs and going to New York to make records.

Charlie's parting words were: "Goodbye, boys. We're gone!"

Soon after, the North Carolina Ramblers boarded a train for Passaic, New Jersey, where they stayed with a childhood friend of Posey. Charlie and Norman took short-term jobs at a railroad car factory and Posey in a textile mill. They were making the money they needed to survive before Charlie took his big step.

HISTORIC RECORDING SESSION

One day, Charlie took off from work and crossed the Hudson River. Illiterate and with a thick, rural, southern accent, Charlie was a stranger in a strange land. He built up all the courage he could muster and walked in, uninvited, to the offices of Columbia Records on West Fifty-ninth Street in midtown Manhattan.

He was determined to land an audition for the North Carolina Ramblers, and he did. Columbia scheduled the group to audition a few days later with Frank Walker, Columbia's A&R (artists and repertoire) man in charge of its "Old Familiar Tunes" series.

At the audition, Charlie, Posey and Norman played "Don't Let Your Deal Go Down Blues." Frank Walker stopped the group after only a few bars. The North Carolina Ramblers sounded different from other old-time bands he had heard in person or on recordings. The trio had the instruments and repertoire of a typical rural string band, but their music was tighter and had an almost jazzy swing. Walker loved their unique sound.

Soon after, on July 27, 1925, the North Carolina Ramblers recorded four songs for Columbia. At the session, Charlie was a bundle of nerves, as were Posey and Norman. According to Kinney Rorrer:

> *They were all terrified when they recorded. Norman said that he was so nervous that the people at Columbia had to send to a pharmacy to get something to calm his nerves. Norman also said that Charlie said that it was a wonder that the sound of the butterflies in his stomach were not heard on the recordings. Norman also said that Charlie swore that he would never record sober again.*

Despite the mental turmoil it caused him, Charlie's moxie paid off. He was an overnight star. The North Carolina Ramblers' debut record, released in

North Carolina Ramblers, Beckley, West Virginia, 1927. Posey Rorer (left), Charlie Poole (center) and Roy Harvey (right). *Photo by Young's Studio, courtesy of the Kinney Rorer Collection.*

September 1925, was a huge hit. "Don't Let Your Deal Go Down Blues" and, on the flip side, "Can I Sleep in Your Barn Tonight Mister" sold a staggering 102,000 copies at a time when 20,000 records sold was considered a hit.

According to Kinney Rorrer, "Poole's crisp, sharp singing style made the band instantly recognizable…The tight, almost chamber music quality to the band set Poole's North Carolina Ramblers apart from the typical string band of the period."

A couple months later, Columbia released a record of the other songs the group recorded in June: "The Girl I Left in Sunny Tennessee" and "I'm the Man That Rode the Mule 'Round the World." The record sold sixty-five thousand copies, another big hit.

FULL-TIME MUSICIAN

In 1926, Charlie Poole and the North Carolina Ramblers went to New York for their second Columbia recording session. Norman Woodlieff, not a rambler by nature, had left the group. To take his place, Charlie had found a guitarist from Beckley, West Virginia, named Roy Harvey. The teetotaling Harvey would record with the Ramblers on almost all future recordings and serve as the group's manager.

During the 1926 session, Columbia offered Charlie an exclusive contract. With his earnings, he bought a new Gibson RB4 Mastertone banjo, a make and model that would become the bluegrass gold standard.

Charlie Poole was a thirty-four-year-old man who had been working in the mills since he was about nine years old. He was thrilled to have the financial freedom to quit millwork and play music full time.

BEST-KNOWN PICKER AND SINGER
IN THE CAROLINAS

During the next few years, Charlie continued to be a major figure in old-time music. According to the 1927 Columbia catalogue:

Charlie Poole is unquestionably the best-known picker and singer in the Carolinas. A dance in North Carolina, Virginia, or Kentucky isn't a

dance unless Charlie and the North Carolina Ramblers supply the pep.
People everywhere dance all night when these favorites supply the music.

About half of what the North Carolina Ramblers recorded were popular songs from before 1905. First composed as orchestral or chamber music, these were funny and sentimental Victorian ballads from the vaudeville stage. Many were by Tin Pan Alley composers. Poole had rearranged them for old-time and given them new, peppy dance rhythms.

Charlie did something similar with ragtime, blues and jazz numbers; he arranged them into his own unique old-time style. The remainder of songs the band recorded were traditional fiddle and banjo tunes.

Fans loved the wide variety of Charlie's songs. He offered nostalgia and old-fashioned themes that people related to while packaging his songs in his own creative and forward-looking style.

Charlie got his songs from phonograph records, traveling vaudeville and minstrel shows, fellow musicians and sheet music. Up until late in his life, he relied on family members to read the lyrics to him. It would not be until he was in his mid-thirties that Lou Emma would teach him to read and write. Until then, Charlie relied on his amazing memory.

STARS ON THE ROAD

From the time the North Carolina Ramblers released their hit record in 1925, Charlie Poole had become a celebrity not to be missed at a live stage show. Crowds were bigger than ever. Even in remote hamlets, the North Carolina Ramblers played to houses packed to the brim.

Charlie was not only a great musician but also a great entertainer. At his shows, he served as the host, cracking jokes and telling stories between songs. Charlie was also a fine dancer and acrobat. He'd leap over a chair placed in the middle of the stage. Audiences laughed and cheered when he'd land on his hands and dance on them with his legs in the air.

Despite his antics on stage, Charlie was very professional. He practiced constantly and demanded his bandmates do the same. He delivered musical excellence, even when he performed in the most remote regions. Even when drunk, he worked to make the show of the highest quality. Once he fell out of his chair while playing at a school graduation. He got right back on the chair and continued playing.

CHARLIE POOLE SPLITS WITH POSEY RORER

When not on the road, Charlie Poole and the North Carolina Ramblers were in the recording studio. The group recorded seven times, with Charlie recording a total of eighty-five songs.

When the North Carolina Ramblers were in New York for their recording sessions, Columbia put them up at a hotel. The men spent days practicing in their room. They had a taste for the nightlife, too. From time to time, they'd venture out into the big city to soak up its sights and sounds.

In 1927, long-brewing tensions between Charlie and Posey broke out into the open. That year, after the North Carolina Ramblers' third New York recording session, Posey quit the group after a bitter business dispute over royalties. Posey accused Charlie of withholding his money and spending it on a drunken spree. Charlie accused Posey of recording without him under the North Carolina Ramblers' name.

For nearly a decade, Charlie and Posey had made music together at home, on the road and in the recording studio. They had become close to each other's families and were related through marriage. Harsh words must have been said because the former partners and close friends never reconciled.

POOLE EYES POP MARKET

In 1928, for Charlie Poole and the North Carolina Ramblers' fourth recording session, Charlie replaced Posey Rorer with fiddler Lonnie Austin. Trained in the Spray community music program, Lonnie was younger and more pop oriented than Posey. Charlie and Roy Harvey preferred the Tin Pan Alley and jazz music of the day to the Appalachian fiddle tunes Posey had favored. Charlie Poole and Roy Harvey welcomed Lonnie Austin into the group.

By the next year, 1929, Charlie was featured in two important catalogues. Photos of the handsome Poole were on the cover of the Columbia's "Old Familiar Tunes" catalogue. The Gibson banjo catalogue featured a smiling Charlie Poole holding his shiny banjo.

Though famous in old-time music circles, Charlie dreamed of expanding his fan base. He hoped that adding the musically versatile Lonnie Austin would help. Charlie yearned to move the group out of its niche in Columbia's country music series and break into pop music.

CHARLIE POOLE WITH THE NORTH CAROLINA RAMBLERS

North Carolina Ramblers, circa 1927. Charlie Poole (left), Posey Rorer (center) and Roy Harvey (right). *[Pf-20001/1254_01] in the John Edwards Memorial Foundation Records, Southern Folklife Collection, the Wilson Library, University of North Carolina at Chapel Hill.*

In 1929, for the group's fifth session at Columbia Records in New York, Charlie arrived intent on recording a more mainstream sound. He brought along an extra fiddler, Odell Smith, as well as pianist Lucy Terry, Roy Harvey's sister. Charlie liked bringing along the added instruments for a fuller, more pop sound.

But Columbia's Frank Walker did not see Charlie Poole as the next Al Jolson. Charlie was more musically sophisticated than many country artists, but he lacked the polish preferred by the mainstream audience. Walker insisted the North Carolina Ramblers stick with the tried-and-true banjo-fiddle-guitar format. Two years earlier, he had allowed Charlie to record songs with piano and mandolin and did not like the results. This time, Walker insisted that Charlie and his group record as a rural old-time trio.

Charlie would not take "no" for an answer. Three days later, he took his group to the Paramount studios and recorded with the instruments he wanted under the name the Highlanders. Two days later, the five musicians went to the Brunswick studios and recorded as the Allegheny Highlanders.

Frank Walker had a keen business sense, but Charlie Poole had musical vision. The five-piece band's use of twin fiddles played in tight unison, combined with Charlie's banjo solo breaks (a technique he borrowed from jazz), foreshadowed a style of music that would emerge more than fifteen years later: bluegrass.

FINAL RECORDINGS

In January and September 1930, the North Carolina Ramblers, led by Charlie, recorded its last two sessions with Columbia. Charlie Poole was on banjo and vocals, Roy Harvey on guitar and Odell Smith on fiddle, replacing Lonnie Austin, who had a conflicting gig with a vaudeville act. Odell Smith, young and from the Spray area, was an admirer of Lonnie Austin and played in a similar style.

At their 1930 sessions, the North Carolina Ramblers made great music, but record sales were poor. The group was competing with other bands that had copied their style. Also, the country had plunged into a financial collapse. Most people had little money to spend on records.

In the fall of 1930, with the Great Depression and declining record sales, Columbia cancelled Charlie Poole's recording contact. He was crushed.

PREMATURE FINALE

About one month later, Charlie picked himself up out of the doldrums. He did a series of live broadcasts on North Carolina and Virginia radio stations. That winter, he went on a thirty-theater tour across West Virginia and Ohio with five musicians. One of them was his son, James, now seventeen and a fine vocalist. The six-piece band performed its sets between reels in movie houses. The moviegoers loved the music so much that when the movie came back on, they booed.

Despite the North Carolina Ramblers' popularity, as the band made its way into Ohio, the crowds thinned. Many people simply could not afford the tickets. Declining attendance, combined with Charlie's increased drinking and several heart seizures along the road, forced the group to end its tour early in Cincinnati and return to Spray.

No longer able to make a living as a musician, Charlie went back to work in the mills. After more than five years as a famous recording artist and performer, he was doing the factory work that he had so eagerly left behind. It was agonizing for Charlie, and his drinking grew worse. Lou Emma, his siblings and his friends tried to cheer him up, but they couldn't lift his spirits.

In February, something did help: a surprise letter from a Hollywood movie company asking him to play for one of its films. In the envelope for him and his bandmates were train tickets to California. Elated by his stroke of good luck, Charlie went out with drinking buddies to celebrate the good news.

The celebration turned into a thirteen-week bender. Lou Emma, Charlie's sister Sarah and other friends and family begged him to stop. Charlie was unable. Some said the final straw was some bad liquor he drank on his last day. On May 21, 1931, two weeks before he was to leave for Hollywood, Charlie lay in his sister's home, dead from a heart attack. He was thirty-nine years old.

Poole left behind devastated fans, musical partners, friends and family. He was a musician with great talent, vision and guts. Virtually every bluegrass musician owes a debt to Charlie Poole.

LEGACY

Kinney Rorrer, Charlie's biographer and great-nephew of Charlie Poole and Posey Rorer, sees Charlie as the "grandfather of bluegrass":

> *Charlie Poole established a template for the core of a bluegrass band: finger-picked banjo, longbow fiddle and heavy guitar runs. Poole's chief legacy was his recording, and thus preserving, the definitive versions of songs such as "The Girl I Left in Sunny Tennessee," "White House Blues" and "If I Lose." Modern bluegrass bands continue to draw on the wealth of material first recorded by Poole.*

But unlike most modern bluegrass bands, Charlie Poole lived the words he sang. Songs such as "Take a Drink On Me" and "He Rambled" described Charlie's own experiences. His lifestyle cut his time short, but his legacy has been a lasting one. On one of his records, Charlie sang, "You'll talk about me when I'm dead and gone." He was right.

Kinney Rorrer's Favorite Charlie Poole Songs

"Don't Let Your Deal Go Down Blues"
"There Will Come a Time"
"White House Blues"

Essential Charlie Poole CDs

Essential Charlie Poole box set
Old Time Songs: Charlie Poole and the North Carolina Ramblers, Volumes 1 and 2
You Ain't Talkin' to Me: Charlie Poole and the Roots of Country Music box set

Charlie Poole's North Carolina

Charlie Poole Festival (Eden)
Haw River Historical Museum, small Charlie Poole exhibit

2

TOMMY JARRELL

COMMUNITY

At-a-Glance

DATES: *1901–1985*
INSTRUMENTS: *Fiddle, banjo*
MUSIC STYLE: *Old-time*
HOME: *Round Peak and Toast in Surry County, North Carolina*
AWARDS: *National Heritage Fellowship from the National Endowment for the Arts*
LEGACY: *Tommy Jarrell was the grand old man of the Round Peak style who influenced so many people that, if one hears old-time music played anywhere in the world, it's likely the Round Peak style. Jarrell was more known than any other old-time musician and recorded more LPs. His fiddle now resides at the Smithsonian Institution in Washington, D.C.*

MUSIC, LIQUOR AND STORIES

Thomas Jefferson Jarrell was born in 1901 into a close-knit family of Scots-Irish descent in the Round Peak community of northern Surry County. The Jarrells were known for excellent music, stories and homemade liquor. Their farm lay at the foot of Fisher Peak, a mountain straddling the North Carolina–Virginia state line.

Tommy Jarrell, Mount Airy, North Carolina, 1980. *Photo by Robert Merritt.*

Tommy was the second oldest of Susan Amburn Jarrell's eleven children and the most musical of the lot. Susan Jarrell cooked, tended the garden and worked the fields. Her husband, Ben Jarrell (1880–1946), often pursued work off the farm. For much of Tommy's childhood, his father ran a small store in Round Peak. Ben Jarrell was also a gifted musician and a moonshiner. He made whiskey from the water of the creeks dotting the area and sometimes traveled away from home to make liquor.

Grandfather Rufus Jarrell (1840–1921) was a Confederate war veteran and a tough taskmaster. Tommy remembered following him everywhere "like a puppy dog." Beginning at age eight, Tommy worked the fields from sunup until sundown when he wasn't in school, with a short break for supper. Grandfather Jarrell made sure Tommy and his siblings had chores when it rained.

The Jarrell family's hard work on the farm provided them with enough food to eat. They grew most of it, including corn, beans and apples. They also raised tobacco. Though steak and ham were rare treats, the Jarrells hunted rabbit and squirrel. If ever the harvest was lean, Tommy's father or grandfather would make and sell liquor.

HOMEMADE ENTERTAINMENT IN ROUND PEAK

The Round Peak community where Tommy grew up was tightknit. Everyone knew one another, and many people were related through marriage. Folks helped one another in times of need. One winter, during the great flu of 1918, when Tommy and his family had the deadly virus, a neighbor came each day to chop firewood, milk the cows and leave milk and other food on the porch.

The lifestyle of Round Peak was non-materialistic and down-to-earth. Young Tommy lived in a world without cars or electricity, with little influence from commercial culture. Folks' sense of satisfaction and well-being came from the fruits of hard labor, the bonds of friendship and the joys of homemade entertainment. The residents of Round Peak made their own fun.

Music and dancing filled community life. Tommy's father and his brother, Charlie Jarrell (1874–1943), were two of the area's best fiddlers. There were a lot of dances around Round Peak, and the Jarrells played at many. Most of what they played were tunes from days gone by. They learned them from old-timers in the region and added their own twists. Ben and Charlie Jarrell's music was intense, rhythmic and perfect for dancing.

The dances were held in people's homes. A fiddler and a banjoist played in the doorway between two rooms. People cleared furniture and rolled up the rugs to create a dance floor. The dances, like the tunes, had been handed down over time. There were different styles of square dancing, including cotillions and Virginia reels, which had been enjoyed for generations in the South, coming from the British Isles and continental Europe. Tommy and his family would listen as the caller shouted out, "Hands up, circle to the left, half way and back. Then swing your partner and promenade!"

Tommy and his siblings also enjoyed music and dancing at the end of "workings" on farms. Throughout the year, people helped one another with tasks that were too big to do alone, such as barn raising, shucking endless ears of corn and peeling hundreds of apples. At the end of a long day's work, to reward everyone for their labor, the host would throw a party with good food, music and dancing.

Holidays and special events were also times for music and dance. The Christmas holiday was party season. For two weeks, people would go from house to house for "Breaking Up Christmas." Music and dancing started in the afternoon and lasted until the wee hours of the morning. Each Easter, Tommy's father and uncle Charlie played music on Fisher Peak. To mark the end of the school year, the Jarrells and other musicians played at what were called "school breakings." Fiddlers led processions of children out of schoolhouses and around the school grounds.

A Song Called "Reuben"

In 1909, when he was eight years old, Tommy learned to play the banjo. His parents had hired a neighbor, Baugie Cockerham, to help with their crop. One day, Tommy and Baugie were out in the meadow minding the grazing steers. Baugie played the song "Reuben" on his banjo and then taught it to Tommy. Like other Round Peak banjoists, Baugie played in the African-derived clawhammer style, stroking down across the strings.

About a year later, Tommy's father bought his son his own banjo. Grandfather Rufus told him he should have brought Tommy a mattock for hoeing instead of a banjo so he could get more work done.

But after a few months of hearing Tommy play, even Rufus Jarrell admired his grandson's musical progress. Tommy spent many hours playing the banjo behind his father's fiddling. Two years later, in 1911, at age ten, Tommy was good enough to play for his first dance, strumming banjo while his father fiddled.

Fiddling Like His Father

When Tommy was almost thirteen, he decided he wanted to play the fiddle like his daddy. Having left school around the seventh grade, Tommy was working on the farm full time and eager for outlets from work.

For years, he had intently watched his father's fiddling, soaking in the tunes, body movements and rhythmic bowing techniques. He absorbed his father's old-fashioned style. It used "rocking the bow," in which the bow made short rocking motions to make as many strings as possible vibrate together.

Ben Jarrell bought Tommy his first fiddle from a neighbor for five dollars. Tommy was excited to follow in his father's footsteps. The rest of his life, most of the tunes Tommy would play were ones he'd learned from his dad.

Around age fifteen, Tommy was asked to fill in for his father at a dance. There were a lot of banjoists around Round Peak but not many fiddlers, and another one was always welcome. Waiting for him when he showed up at the dance was the most respected banjoist in the area: Charlie Lowe.

Mentored by Charlie Lowe

Many people point to Charlie Lowe (1878–1964) as the key figure in creating the intense and driving Round Peak style of old-time banjo playing. His banjo style helped to shape the distinctive Round Peak band sound that is now known around the world. All Round Peak banjoists that followed would interpret Charlie Lowe's playing style.

Lowe was a couple years older than Tommy's father and was Ben Jarrell's regular partner. The first time they played together at a dance, Tommy and Charlie clicked—not surprising, since Tommy played the fiddle much like his dad. Charlie Lowe enjoyed encouraging younger musicians and loved mentoring Ben Jarrell's eldest son.

Charlie Lowe became Tommy's most frequent playing partner at local dances. For almost half a century, Lowe was both an excellent musical partner for Tommy and a kind-hearted person who modeled fine behavior. Lowe was unusually generous, even by the standards of Round Peak. When Tommy or others were visiting, if it was mealtime, Lowe would invite everyone to eat with his family.

Playing "Little Maggie" for Julie

One day, when Tommy was in his mid-teens on his way back from the mill on horseback, he saw some of Uncle Charlie's young children running toward him crying. Their sister, Tommy's cousin Julie—in his words, "fourteen and just as pretty and nice as she could be"—had been helping her mother cook dinner in their wood stove.

Pouring kerosene on the wood to revive the flame, Cousin Julie caught fire. A doctor who visited pronounced her burns too severe to survive.

After the accident, as she lay in bed not far from death, Julie asked Tommy to play "Little Maggie" on his banjo. Tommy played the song, and he played it the best he ever had in his life, filled with feeling and love. The song comforted Julie and lifted her spirits. Tommy always remembered that day and always felt that playing "Little Maggie" for Julie was the hardest thing he'd ever done.

YOUNG FIDDLER LEARNING OLD SONGS

All through his teens, Tommy played his fiddle at dances in people's homes and barns. He played two or three times a week accompanied by Charlie Lowe on banjo. Tommy was a quick learner, always eager to pick up new songs.

Tommy and Charlie Lowe played Round Peak favorites, such as "Drunken Hiccups" (also known as "Jack of Diamonds"), a tune that Ben Jarrell taught to Tommy. Ben and Charlie Jarrell liked preserving the old ways in music and in life in general. Some of their songs were from the Civil War era or even before.

Tommy also liked the old songs, and he learned them in unexpected ways. One day, as he walked down the road to play at a dance, fiddle under his arm, Tommy met a friend of his grandfather. He was a Civil War veteran named Preston "Pet" McKinney (1846–1926). Old Man Pet borrowed Tommy's fiddle and played the old tune "Sail Away Ladies." Tommy asked him to play the tune again. Tommy memorized it on the spot.

TOMMY HEARS AFRICAN AMERICAN MUSIC

When Tommy was growing up more than forty years after the Civil War, not all of the musicians he knew were white. A moderate number of African Americans lived in the Mount Airy area. Many worked at the large granite quarry or on their family farms. Though life in Round Peak and Surry County in general was segregated, Tommy sometimes heard black musicians play, and he liked what he heard.

The Round Peak style of playing got its rhythmic, syncopated flavor in part from the influence of black musicians living in or touring through the area. Tommy remembers an African American banjo player who played for the family when he came to buy whiskey from Ben Jarrell.

Another time, Tommy went to a traveling show in Mount Airy and heard the song "Boll Weevil." The performer was a light-skinned black woman.

He listened intently as she sang: "Boll Weevil told a farmer you better treat me right." Tommy made sure he went back to hear her again so he could learn the enchanting song.

MOONSHINING

In 1918, when Tommy was seventeen years old, his father closed his store in Round Peak and went to Oregon for three years to make whiskey. Ben ended up spending a year and a half in jail, so Tommy, his brother Fred and Grandfather Rufus took charge of the family. Tommy worked the family farm, which was very hard since the land was poor. He tried farming tobacco, but by the time he paid off the fertilizer bill, he was in the red. Around 1920, he decided to pursue what had been a profit-making venture for Jarrell men for generations.

Tommy became a moonshiner, illegal in the state since 1909. Uncle Charlie taught him how to make whiskey, and his grandfather taught him how to proof it. His brother Fred worked with him. Whiskey reaped a good profit, selling for twenty dollars a gallon. For the next several years, Tommy's main source of income was making moonshine.

In 1921, whiskey was at the root of a near family tragedy. One evening, nineteen-year-old Tommy and his brother Fred had a violent fight with their uncle Charlie Jarrell, a mean drunk. After Uncle Charlie bloodied Fred's head with the butt of a shotgun, Tommy hit his uncle with a pistol. Uncle Charlie cut Tommy's head and neck with his knife.

When, the next day, Uncle Charlie took out a warrant for his nephews' arrest, Tommy and Fred crossed the state line to stay with family in Lambsburg, Virginia. Within months, feelings had cooled down on both sides, and Uncle Charlie dropped the arrest warrant. But Tommy and Fred never forgot what the doctor in Lambsburg told them: Uncle Charlie's knife had missed Tommy's jugular by an inch.

FINDING ZACH PAYNE

Tommy and Fred stayed in Virginia. They worked and boarded at the home of a family friend, banjo picker Charlie Barnett Lowe (1872–1924, no

Tommy Jarrell, Toast, North Carolina, 1984. *Photo by Alice Gerard, [Pf-20006/52, scan 26] in the Alice Gerrard Collection, Southern Folklife Collection, the Wilson Library, University of North Carolina at Chapel Hill.*

relation to Charlie Lowe). Charlie had a pretty daughter, Nina, who caught Tommy's eye. In between raising crops and making whiskey, Tommy learned tunes from Charlie Barnett Lowe and other musicians in Carroll County.

Tommy heard about an eighty-two-year-old Civil War veteran named Zach Payne. He'd played the fife during the war and was still one of the best fiddlers in Carroll County. Tommy was determined to meet him. One day, Tommy and Fred set out to the Payne farm.

There they found Old Man Payne sitting under an apple tree. Tommy asked him if he'd go to his house, get his fiddle and play a tune for him. When Payne refused, Tommy offered him a half pint of his best homemade whiskey. By the time he got to his house, Payne was in a mood to oblige. He played two old fiddle tunes that he'd learned during the Civil War: "Flatwoods" and "Devil in the Strawstack."

Tommy learned both.

A BLUNT PROPOSAL

In 1923, when Tommy was twenty-two years old, he proposed to Charlie Barnett Lowe's daughter Nina. According to Tommy's nephew Thomas Reavis Lyons, Tommy had an interesting talk with her: "Nina, we'll get married if you want to. But I'll tell you right now, I make whiskey, I play poker and I go to dances, make music and I don't know whether I'll ever quit that or not."

Nina accepted Tommy's proposal. They had a solid forty-three-year marriage.

In the early years of their marriage, they lived with Nina's parents in Virginia. After the Lowes died in 1924, Tommy and Nina moved to the Toast community outside Mount Airy to live with Tommy's parents. In 1921, Tommy's family had moved there from Round Peak, after his father returned from Oregon and decided to open a new dry goods store.

Toast was located near where many of Mount Airy's African Americans lived. Jim Rawley, a member of a well-known black family in the area, would sing "Ryland Spencer" every Sunday morning as he walked down the road past Tommy's window. Tommy heard the song and was determined to learn that one, too.

ROAD GRADER

In 1925, Tommy decided to quit making liquor and playing poker and started working with the North Carolina State Highway Department as a road grader. He would have the job for the next forty-one years. Tommy and Nina had three children: Ardena (Dena), born in 1925; Clarence (Wayne), born in 1927; and Benjamin Franklin (B.F.), born in 1933. Tommy, Nina and their children had enough food to eat and clothes to wear, though they lived simply, never owning a telephone or car.

Music continued to be part of the life of the Jarrell clan. In 1927, Tommy's father joined a group that recorded nine 78rpm records for Gennett Records. The group was called Da Costa Woltz's Southern Broadcasters. Woltz, a promoter of patent medicines and the future mayor of nearby Galax, Virginia, recruited Ben Jarrell because Ben was known as one of the region's best fiddlers. Also in the group was banjoist Frank Jenkins and a child ukulele player, Price Goodson. Da Costa Woltz's Southern Broadcasters didn't sell many records, but the fact that the group had recorded would, years later, change Tommy's life.

Throughout the time he worked as a road grader, from 1925 to 1966, Tommy practiced his fiddle after work and played at holiday dances. His repertoire had changed little since the 1920s. Charlie Lowe wanted Tommy to compete with him in the area's numerous fiddlers' contests, but Tommy never wanted to stay up late on weeknights, when many of the contests were held, as he needed to get up early each morning for work.

In 1948, Surry County's old-time music and dance scene was boosted by the launch of a local radio station, WPAQ. The station was rare in its commitment to the area's music traditions. WPAQ validated and preserved the community's music by giving residents the chance to perform live on the air.

It's not clear how often Round Peak musicians performed on WPAQ in those early days. There's some evidence that the Round Peak style was already considered old-fashioned by the late 1940s, '50s and '60s, when bluegrass ruled. By 1948, Uncle Charlie and Ben Jarrell had both passed away, but Tommy and Charlie Lowe sometimes played on WPAQ. Tommy went right on playing music the old way.

INSTRUMENTAL MUSIC REVIVAL

In 1966, at age sixty-five, Tommy retired from his job with a good pension, benefits and more time to play music. Only a year later, Nina passed away. Charlie Lowe, having died three years earlier, was also gone. In 1967, Tommy was living alone in his modest white house. Though he had family living nearby, he missed Nina tremendously.

But Tommy would not be lonely for long. Soon would begin a series of serendipitous events that would put him in the national old-time music spotlight.

By 1967, Doc Watson and other authentic southern folk musicians had been touring the country for several years, performing for crowds at festivals, on college campuses and in coffeehouses and concert halls. The commercial folk boom in the late 1950s, launched by groups like the Kingston Trio, had waned, giving way to musicians like Joan Baez and Bob Dylan.

At the heart of the baby boom, there were more young people than ever before, and many were interested in folk music. These folk fans were mostly well-educated college graduates from urban areas outside the South who were eager to dig deeply into the roots of the songs Dylan and Baez sang.

Many of these diehards were serious musicians who were interested in instrumental old-time music. The focus of the vocally oriented folk revival of the 1950s had been listening to music and singing along. The old-time diehards of the late '60s were more interested in playing the music themselves.

Creating this type of music involved playing with small groups of friends. Typically, a bunch of musicians sat around and jammed, sharing songs. Prized above all was authenticity and quality. Sometimes people got up to dance. The music, the dancing, the friendships—connections were profound. For many, the experience was a balm to the spirit.

TOMMY MEETS ALAN JABBOUR

One such instrumental old-time musician was a classically trained violinist and PhD student at Duke University named Alan Jabbour. He had a passion for playing southern fiddle tunes and for learning from authentic southern masters. Jabbour was doing research on folklore and folk songs and making field recordings of elderly old-time fiddlers. With other young revivalists in the Durham area, Jabbour co-founded the Hollow Rock String Band.

In the summer of 1967—about a year after Tommy retired and six months after Nina died—Jabbour attended the Old Fiddlers' Convention in Galax, Virginia, one of the longest-running and largest old-time and bluegrass events in the nation.

At Galax, a man approached Jabbour and introduced himself as B.F. Jarrell. B.F. had read a feature article on Jabbour's fiddle-tune collecting and recognized Jabbour from the photos. B.F. told Jabbour that his father was one of the best old-time fiddlers around and was the son of Ben Jarrell of Da Costa Woltz's Southern Broadcasters. B.F. offered to introduce Jabbour to his father when his dad came up to the festival the next day.

Jabbour and Tommy hit it off from the start. Jabbour instantly accepted Tommy's invitation to come visit. When the festival ended that Sunday, on their way home to Durham, Jabbour and his wife stopped by Toast. Tommy welcomed them with open arms. Months later, in the spring of 1968, Jabbour returned to Toast several times with his tape recorder. Tommy was pleased to record.

During the recording sessions, Jabbour recognized that he was not just listening to another old guy playing old-time music. This was a superb musician with a unique style on both banjo and fiddle. The style was powerful and expressive. It was rhythmic and syncopated. What made it so captivating was that Tommy's style, along with his repertoire, came from another era.

Excited by what he was hearing, Jabbour told other old-time fans he knew about this remarkable musician who welcomed young musicians into his home. A handful of other musicians from Jabbour's circle began to visit Jarrell and other Surry County old-timers. Jabbour and his friends were thrilled to discover a repertoire of hundreds of old-time tunes they'd never heard. Tommy and his musician buddies were excited to have such a receptive audience.

Jabbour and his friends were discovering unique styles of playing. Recalls Jabbour, "It was a musical revelation sitting on the vine, but no one had previously been paying attention."

For Jabbour and his friends, discovering the music of Tommy Jarrell and other authentic southern old-timers was more than an eye-opening musical discovery:

> It was a cultural revolution…something larger than music. It was a discovery of who your neighbors were. We saw the people we were visiting not as hillbillies but as people whose artistic resources could transform us and everyone around us.

In the summer of 1968, Jabbour, doctorate in hand, took an academic post in Los Angeles, launching his distinguished career. He spent most of it at the Library of Congress, becoming the first director of the library's American Folklife Center.

The fact that Jabbour was so impressed by Jarrell caught the attention of old-time music fans from around North Carolina and the nation. After graduating from Duke, Jabbour never lived in North Carolina again, but he had made an important discovery in Tommy Jarrell that would have a huge impact on the state's old-time world and the old-time world everywhere.

FAUROT, FREEMAN AND COUNTY RECORDS

During the summer of 1967, another old-time aficionado met Tommy at the Galax Fiddlers' Convention. His name was Charles Faurot. A graduate of Andover and Yale, Faurot was an amateur banjo player and record collector who, as a hobby, had been making field recordings of rural southern musicians.

For years, Faurot had been traveling south to the Galax–Mount Airy region. He loved the square dances, the Galax Fiddlers' Convention and the homespun programming of WPAQ. He adored the incredible music.

In 1967, Faurot was working with County Records in New York City, the brainchild of founder and owner Dave Freeman. Faurot convinced Freeman that County should produce new field recordings of living musicians. Faurot told him that he knew where to find great musicians down South.

At the 1967 Galax convention, Charles Faurot, Dave Freeman and Rich Nevins (another old-time enthusiast from New York) bumped into Oscar Jenkins. Collectors of vintage old-time records, the three New Yorkers were immediately drawn to Jenkins. In 1927, Oscar's father, Frank, had recorded with Ben Jarrell in Da Costa Woltz's Southern Broadcasters. The New Yorkers asked Oscar if he had any old 78rpms of his father's old group.

Oscar didn't but suggested that they visit Tommy Jarrell to see if he had any of the records. Freeman and Nevins made the short drive south. Though Tommy didn't get out any old 78s, he did something better. He and Oscar Jenkins performed for Freeman and Nevins, who went straight back to Faurot to tell him they were blown away by what they'd heard.

The three New Yorkers spent the next days recording Tommy and Oscar, along with Fred Cockerham (1905–1980).

Fred Cockerham was an outstanding banjoist and fiddler from Round Peak. He was the only one of all the Round Peak musicians who had pursued a professional music career, performing on live radio shows and at festivals and fiddlers' conventions. Tommy and Oscar knew Fred well. In their youth, Tommy and Fred had played music together. Their sound was still tight five decades later.

The recordings of Jenkins, Cockerham and Jarrell led to the release of two 1968 County Records LPs: "Down to the Cider Mill" and "Stay All Night and Don't Go Home." A concert tour of the Northeast followed. In the summer of 1968, the three southerners performed at the Newport Folk Festival in Rhode Island. On the way home, they stopped off at the New Jersey home of friends of Dave Freeman to play a house concert.

County also produced three clawhammer banjo LPs, which became bestsellers. The first one did not include Tommy, but *Claw Hammer Banjo*, Volumes 2 and 3, did. These recordings, as well as "Down to the Cider Mill" and "Stay All Night," had a huge impact on folk music fans. The albums were authentic. They were intense.

RAY ALDEN, THE CONNECTOR

A young banjo player and math teacher from New York City named Ray Alden loved these albums. Alden had attended the house concert in New Jersey where Tommy, Fred and Oscar performed on their way home from Newport. Alden had been astounded by what he'd heard and had left the concert determined to learn all he could about the musicians and their music.

The next summer, in 1969, Alden drove down to Surry County to take banjo lessons from Fred Cockerham. He also visited with Tommy at his house, enjoying his music, humor and hospitality. Alden recorded their music sessions and, after he went back up North, used them to practice his new, authentic southern style.

During the summers, Alden continued to visit Surry County, sometimes bringing along friends from the New York area. Alden was a warm person who found his passion in the music, people and culture of Surry County. He eased the way for many others to follow him into Tommy's world.

In 1972, Alden wrote an influential article for *Sing Out!* magazine called "Music from Round Peak." In the article, he talked about his summer visits to Round Peak and his friendships with the musicians there, focusing on Jarrell. In the article, Alden coined the term "Round Peak music." Young, urban folk fans read the article and decided to follow in Ray Alden's footsteps.

PILGRIMAGES TO TOMMY'S

Young people began to flock to Surry County. Some people heard about Tommy through Alden's article. Others heard Tommy play on one of the County LPs. Others heard of Tommy at music festivals or through the powerful old-time grapevine. People came from around the country and from as far away as Germany, Australia and Japan. Over the years, thousands of young music pilgrims came to Surry County to learn from Tommy Jarrell, the grand old man of the Round Peak style.

The young, urban enthusiasts flocking to Tommy were digging deep into authentic old-time music. The more archaic the music, the better. They wanted to get as far away from modern, homogenized culture as possible, and with Tommy Jarrell, they'd hit the mother lode. Even in the 1920s, much of Tommy's repertoire had harkened back to an earlier time, and it had changed little in the decades since. That Tommy had learned some of his

Left to right: Verlen Clifton, Paul Brown, Tommy Jarrell and Chester McMillian, Mount Airy, North Carolina, 1980. *Photo by Robert Merritt.*

tunes directly from Civil War veterans intrigued many of the young pilgrims, whose prior connection to Civil War history had been through textbooks.

The pilgrims loved Tommy's riveting, high-intensity, passionate playing style. Tommy's archaic style of fiddling used old-fashioned and complex bowing techniques that gave the instrument the sound of a band. He kept all the strings busy and vibrating, which made the fiddle sound fuller and richer. He used similar techniques on the banjo.

Tommy's warm, larger-than-life personality also made him a magnet for young people who wanted to meet southern old-time masters. In a community whose musicians welcomed visitors, nobody did it like Tommy. He also had a great sense of humor and often used it to poke fun at himself. Music pilgrim Paul Brown remembered that Tommy, after taking a while to get in tune, would exclaim, "There, the blind hog stumbled upon an acorn!"

In addition, Tommy was highly intelligent and could articulate well to people who wanted to learn what he did on the fiddle and banjo. His verbal talents also made the past come alive through his vivid stories of days gone by in Round Peak.

Though many of the young old-time pilgrims were from outside Tommy's home region, a few were local and rural. One was Kirk Sutphin from nearby

Forsyth County. Kirk's grandfather, from Surry County, had known Tommy in his youth. Growing up, Kirk hadn't paid much attention to old-time music. But he became more interested in Tommy's music after his father bought him one of the County LPs. Kirk soon became one of Tommy's youngest and most eager protégés, learning to emulate Tommy's fiddle and banjo style as well as anyone.

For all of Tommy's protégés, learning to play from him was an experience they treasured. Alan Jabbour describes Tommy as "everyone's favorite uncle" and the relationship between Tommy and his young visitors as

> *a happy thing. Tommy was a great artist with a great personality. That made him a great teacher. He taught by being. An apprenticeship with Tommy Jarrell meant just hanging out, soaking it all up…People would talk about* [it] *the rest of their lives.*

NONSTOP PARTY AT TOMMY'S

The party atmosphere at Tommy's house was like the parties of his youth: great music and dancing, tales of the colorful old days and delicious home cooking. The guest list had changed, with a more diverse flavor to the crowd, but the sense of community and joy that had been so strong years earlier was still there. Ben and Charlie Jarrell and Charlie Lowe were there in spirit.

The young musical pilgrims who yearned for a sense of community—especially one without pretense and materialistic values—had found it beyond their wildest hopes in Surry County. For them, the sense of community at Tommy's was better than what they'd find at a peace rally because these young people were drawn more to music than to politics. It was better than the folk music scene on college campuses and in Greenwich Village because, at Tommy's, visitors could hear and feel the music in the company of the Appalachian folk who had made it and lived it for generations.

Often on a Saturday night, there'd be a happy crowd of about fifty people in Tommy's small house and yard. People walked in through Tommy's kitchen, where folks would be flatfoot dancing and clogging. Talking, joking and roars of laughter filled the air. Beans cooked on the stove, and homemade cakes and pies sat on the kitchen table. In the living room, Tommy sat on his green sofa, fiddling with intensity. To pilgrim Mike

Seeger, Tommy—by doing intricate bow work with his right hand—seemed to be playing three times the notes he was playing with his left.

The pilgrims found Tommy's music intoxicating and soaked it in as best they could. Tommy gave everyone a chance to play, but he had the most patience with the better players. Many of the pilgrims were already accomplished old-time musicians. They had come south to pick up the intricacies of Round Peak rhythms and bowing techniques.

Tommy and his relatives and musician friends welcomed the young pilgrims with open arms and open hearts. They enjoyed the company and attention. They realized their music traditions had value.

Some of Surry County's musicians who came to these parties at Tommy's house were members of the influential area string band the Camp Creek Boys: Kyle Creed, Fred Cockerham, Verlen Clifton, Earnest East, Paul Sutphin, Ronald Collins and Benton Flippen. Other Surry County musicians included Dix Freeman, Chester McMillian, Robert Sykes, Gilmer Woodruff, Frank and Ginger Bode and Mac Snow.

Though weekends were the busiest times at Tommy's, on almost every night of the week, Tommy would mentor a young person at his house. Tommy invited the young people to stay over if they needed a place, though he expected some help with chores. He got frustrated only once with one of his visitors. To dissuade him from staying too long, and as a joke, Tommy put a sign at the front of his house: "First Two Nights Free and After That $20 Per Night."

Some people stayed in Surry County for a week and some for a lifetime. Pilgrims would stay with friends or acquaintances who had moved to the area or at Tommy's house, in motels, at campsites in state parks or at cheap rental houses.

Pilgrims who stayed in North Carolina have made lasting contributions to the state's culture. These have included David Holt, the topic of chapter six; Alice Gerrard, who would become the founder of the *Old-Time Herald* in Durham; Wayne Erbsen, who would start Native Ground Books and Records in Asheville; Barry Poss, who would begin Sugar Hill Records in Durham; Andy Cahan, who would become an influential musician and field recordist; George Holt, who would become the director of the North Carolina Arts Council's Folklife Program; and Joe Newberry, who would become chief communications officer for the North Carolina Department of Cultural Resources.

Paul Brown—a banjo enthusiast who grew up in the New York suburbs—was another pilgrim who stayed. When he was a child, Brown's

Tommy Jarrell and Andy Cahan, Toast, North Carolina, 1984. *Photo by Alice Gerrard, [Pf-20006/52, scan 4] in the Alice Gerrard Collection, Southern Folklife Collection, the Wilson Library, University of North Carolina at Chapel Hill.*

mother, who came from old Virginia stock, had sung him old southern folk songs. During his years at Oberlin College, eager to learn more about the southern soundscape of his childhood, he decided to head south with his banjo to see what he could discover. Through Ray Alden, he met Tommy. In 1980, Brown got an apprenticeship grant from the National Endowment of the Arts to study the banjo with Tommy.

After the apprenticeship, Paul Brown stayed in the area, working all week in factories so he could play music in the evenings and attend dances and fiddlers' conventions on the weekends. He became close friends with Tommy and other Round Peak musicians and their families. Over the years, Paul would work his way up the ladder in the radio world, beginning at WPAQ in Mount Airy, going on to WFDD in Winston-Salem and finally becoming a lead newscaster, reporter and producer for National Public Radio in Washington, D.C. All the while, he kept playing old-time music with his friends in Surry County.

LEGACY

In addition to the scores of people Tommy interacted with who made the pilgrimage to his home, he also influenced people through his performances outside Surry County. Among those he toured with during the 1970s and '80s were Mike Seeger, Blanton Owen and Chester McMillian. Tommy traveled the nation, appearing at almost every major folk festival, as well as at coffeehouses, college campuses and music camps. He influenced so many people that, if one hears old-time music played anywhere in the world, it's likely the Round Peak style.

For a man who lived a simple life out of the public view until he was sixty-five, Tommy gained recognition he never expected. In 1982, he received one of the first National Heritage Fellowships from the National Endowment for the Arts. He is better known and has recorded more LPs than any other old-time musician. He appeared on British television and was the subject of two documentaries. He was featured in *Newsweek*, and in 1985, when he died at age eighty-four, his obituary appeared in the *New York Times*. Tommy Jarrell's fiddle now resides at the Smithsonian Institution in Washington, D.C.

Some of Tommy's Favorite Songs

"Breaking Up Christmas"
"Drunken Hiccups" ("Jack of Diamonds")
"John Brown's Dream"
"Sally Ann"

Essential Tommy Jarrell CDs

Clawhammer Banjo, Volumes 1–3 (County Records)
June Apple
The Legacy of Tommy Jarrell, Volumes 1–3
Tommy and Fred: Best Fiddle-Banjo Duets

Tommy Jarrell's Surry County

Mount Airy Blue Grass and Old-Time Fiddlers Convention

Mount Airy Museum of Regional History, Tommy Jarrell exhibit

Old-Time Music Heritage Hall at the Earl Theater (Mount Airy): The theater has an exhibit on Tommy and other Round Peak musicians.

Tommy Jarrell Festival (Mount Airy)

WPAQ's *Merry Go-Round*: This show at the Earl Theater in Mount Airy is the second oldest currently running live radio program in the country.

Tommy Jarrell Documentaries

My Old Fiddle
Sprout Wings and Fly

3

JOE THOMPSON

STAYING POWER

At-a-Glance

⟡

DATES: 1918–2012
INSTRUMENTS: Fiddle
MUSIC STYLE: Old-time
HOME: Efland and Mebane, North Carolina
AWARDS: Brown-Hudson Award, North Carolina Folk Heritage Award,
  National Heritage Fellowship
LEGACY: From a respected family of musicians, Joe Thompson was the last
  African American old-time musician in North Carolina who learned
  from a family tradition dating back to the nineteenth century. He was
  also probably the last African American old-time musician in the United
  States. Because of Joe Thompson's outstanding musicianship and grit,
  his family's music will be played at coffeehouses and concert halls for
  years to come.

JOE'S GRANDFATHER ROBERT, BORN A SLAVE

Joseph Aquilla Thompson was born in 1918 near Efland in northern
Orange County. Music was in the air and in his DNA. To understand the
special life that lay ahead for Joe, let's take a long look backward.

Joe Thompson, Mebane, North Carolina, 2010. *Photo by Daniel Coston.*

According to Thompson family lore, in 1849, Joe Thompson's grandfather Robert was born into slavery. He grew up on a plantation near Leasburg in Caswell County, likely owned by a man named Walter Thompson. As a young boy, Robert worked there—an expanse of land filled with tobacco, wheat and corn. Around him lay farmland, forests and rolling hills.

After Emancipation, fourteen-year-old Robert, along with the other slaves, received two gifts from his master: land and the Thompson name. Robert left his slave quarters and walked with his parents and siblings to his new house. It was down the way, on a road today called Thompson Road.

As a young man, Robert married a local woman named Kate Nelson. Nine years his junior, she'd also been born a slave. Robert and Kate settled in nearby Person County in Bushy Fork Township. Robert was a diligent man devoted to his family. He and Kate raised eleven boys and one girl. The family worked from sunrise to sunset farming their land.

Robert Thompson loved music. As a child, he likely soaked in the lively sounds of the fiddle and banjo played in the slave quarters and at the master's house. Sundays and holidays were likely the days he heard music the most, when slaves would release the tensions of their grueling workweek and enjoy intense, rhythmic music and dancing.

The fiddle was from Europe, but slaves had played it in the South since colonial days. At white dances, slaves played fiddle tunes their masters had taught them. To entertain themselves, slaves had enjoyed their own "Negro jigs," which had a more African flavor.

As a free man, Robert heard blacks play fiddles and banjos at local square dances, which blacks called "frolics." He loved unwinding with friends, family and neighbors. He danced energetic reels to fiddle and banjo tunes. Robert may have played the fiddle; he did encourage his sons to become musicians. Music was a valued skill. Slaves who played instruments were treated better. Now that blacks were free, musicians were still well respected.

The most musical of Robert's ten children were Jacob (b. 1876), John Arch (b. 1879) and Walter Eugene (b. 1882).

JOE'S FATHER, FIDDLER JOHN ARCH THOMPSON

Robert's son John Arch—Joe Thompson's father—played the banjo and fiddle. The fiddle was his main instrument. He learned to play as a young boy, likely from an old fiddler named Emp Wright, who was probably black or mulatto. John Arch learned to play the fiddle as well or better than anyone.

John Arch and his brothers Jake and Walter took music making very seriously. They practiced all the time. John Arch focused on fiddle and his brothers on banjo. John Arch was disciplined in everything he did. Blacks couldn't afford to mess up. Being as good as whites wasn't good enough. He needed to be better.

Sometime between 1880 and 1900, John Arch and his siblings moved with their parents about thirteen miles south, to northern Orange County. There, the large Thompson family settled on farmland in a remarkable township called Cedar Grove.

Cedar Grove was a community of tobacco farmers, about half of them black and half white. Many blacks owned land, and blacks and whites had about the same amount of money and lived similar lifestyles. People of both races spent time together and generally felt comfortable with one another.

Music was even more integrated in Cedar Grove than in most places in North Carolina. Black and white musicians played at community events, such as barn raisings and corn shuckings. While the tobacco cured, they swapped songs and techniques.

In the early 1900s, John Arch and Jake—sometimes accompanied by Walter—were musicians of choice for black and white dances. While blacks called them "frolics," whites called them "square dances." The music and the dancing were largely the same, though the black musicians generally played in a more rhythmic and syncopated style.

Around 1904, at about age twenty-five, John Arch married Rosa Crisp (1883–1960). "Rosie" was a pious, nurturing woman. John Arch's firmness and Rosie's warmth mixed well to create a strong home life.

Around this time, Robert got sick and died before meeting any of his grandchildren. The family buried Robert on a hill not far from the plantation where he was born. It was a huge loss for the family, but they were determined to carry forth his discipline, strong character and love of music.

During the fallow season between Thanksgiving and Easter, John Arch and his brothers often played six times a week—three for white dances and three for African American ones. The fall was busy music-making time, after corn shuckings. Between Christmas and New Year's, the Thompson brothers played for a dance almost every night.

The typical dance was in the two front rooms of a private home, with the furniture cleared. Folks invited one another to the dance with "hands up eight and don't be late!" John Arch and Jake would sit in the doorway between the two rooms and play the old-time songs. Typically, each room would have an "eight-hand set" dance, which had four couples dancing. Sixteen people would pack the small house, as the sounds of tapping feet, laughing couples and soul-stirring music rose from open windows into the night sky.

John Arch and his brothers played songs from everywhere; to them, there were no racial barriers. They played fiddle instrumentals common to the white old-time tradition, such as "Soldier's Joy." Other songs they played were popular Tin Pan Alley tunes of the day, such as "Buffalo Gals." They also played and sang old-time songs typical of African Americans in the Piedmont, such as "Dona Got a Ramblin' Mind." Other songs in the Thompson repertoire—such as "Pumpkin Pie"—were played in the Piedmont by both blacks and whites and came from early minstrel days.

From 1830 to 1910, minstrel music was hugely popular around the country. Crowds by the hundreds packed into spaces large and small to see the shows. Minstrel songs featured performers in blackface playing the banjo. The skits lampooned blacks as simpletons on plantations. Beginning in the late 1800s, many offended urban blacks turned away from banjo and fiddle music. In the cities, blacks danced to the piano and ragtime and, by the 1910s, to the guitar and blues.

But in northern Orange County—an insular rural area—old-time banjo and fiddle music hung on. John Arch and his brothers loved the music they played and were known for it. Their world was focused not on the hip fashions of the city but on raising tobacco and playing their banjo and fiddle tunes.

When not farming or playing music, John Arch helped Rosie take care of their growing family. By 1916, the couple had five children under age nine: Effie, Katie May, Chesley, Jethro and newborn baby Nathaniel.

JOE THOMPSON BORN INTO MUSIC

Two years later, on December 9, 1918, when John Arch was almost forty, he and Rosie welcomed into the world the sixth of their seven children: Joseph Aquilla Thompson. In 1924, Joe's little brother Robert was born, and the family of nine was complete.

By 1920, the family had moved about six miles south to Efland in Cheeks Township, still in northern Orange County. Hillsborough was about four miles east and Mebane about six miles west. In Efland, John Arch and Rosie owned a 161-acre farm with twelve springs. The Thompsons grew tobacco as a cash crop and raised their own animals and vegetables. Caring and generous, they gave two acres of their farm to the school board for an elementary school for African American children.

Growing up in northern Orange County, Joe and his siblings were surrounded by music. At home and in the fields, Rosie sang to them classic spirituals, such as "Oil in My Vessel." John Arch played his fiddle every night. Uncles Jake and Walter visited with their banjos.

Many times while lying in bed, little Joe heard music floating from miles across the fields. In the early 1920s, country life was even quieter than it is today, and sounds traveled far.

In mid-summer—as early as three o'clock in the morning, when farmers were getting ready to prime tobacco—Joe would hear his father and a neighbor making music. In late summer, Joe would fall asleep listening to farmers from miles away sitting at their tobacco barns, playing their fiddles or banjos to keep themselves awake as they fed fires to cure their crops.

During the day, throughout the year, Joe heard his neighbor singing. In a documentary on Joe's life, he later recalled:

Joe and Odell Thompson, Mebane, North Carolina, 1988. *Photo by Nancy Kalow, [P4705] in the Tommy Thompson Collection, Southern Folklife Collection, the Wilson Library, University of North Carolina at Chapel Hill.*

We had a neighbor...Gene McCauley. He was a white fellow. And he stayed across there about half a mile. And he sang this particular song every day, especially if it was a beautiful sunshiny day... "I Shall Not Be Moved." And I thought he could sing it so well.

Joe was also surrounded by the music-making of his older brothers and cousin. Joe's oldest brother, Chesley, was a dance caller and fiddler. Jethro played guitar. Nate, about two and a half years older than Joe, played banjo. Joe's first cousin Odell was Uncle Walter's son. He was about seven years Joe's senior and played fiddle and guitar.

When John Arch moved from Cedar Grove to Efland, he was no longer living as close to his brother Jake, his most regular playing partner. John Arch needed a new partner who lived closer. He looked to someone very close: his seven-year-old son, Nate.

John Arch trained Nate to play clawhammer banjo, an African-derived technique that involved stroking down on the strings. John Arch used an unusual, strict technique to train Nate. As Joe recalled years later in the documentary, "[Daddy] taped [Nate's] hand up so he couldn't play no music. That's what he did to Nate. And he just sit there and clawhammer for two weeks."

The right hand set the rhythm. With his left hand tied up, Nate was forced to make rhythm his focus. It worked. Before long, he became a great playing partner for his dad.

JOE'S FIRST FIDDLE

Joe wanted to do everything Nate did and was jealous that his father had taught Nate to play the banjo. Watching his older brothers and his cousin Odell play instruments, too, he yearned to play "like them grown big boys." He'd been interested in the fiddle since he was a toddler, when he'd sat squirming on the floor every night listening to his father play. When Joe was just three years old, Rosie could see that he wanted to play his daddy's fiddle. But Rosie told her young son not touch his daddy's fiddle. Joe was too small, and he'd break it.

By age five, Joe was pestering his father all the time. But John Arch hung his fiddle high on a wall. As he'd leave the house, he'd tell his son not to mess with his fiddle. Likely, John Arch was using reverse psychology to make sure Joe would. His plan worked. Joe became more determined, and when his father was out, he'd try his best to climb up and get the fiddle. But it was out of reach.

One day, when Joe was in the garden with his mother, her first cousin Jimmy Wagstaff came to visit. Rosie told Jimmy that Joe was driving her crazy asking to play his daddy's fiddle. Cousin Jimmy had a solution. For selling many seed packets, a seed company had awarded him a little fiddle. He would give it to Joe.

Soon after, home from school, Joe walked four miles to Cousin Jimmy's house, carrying an empty flour sack his mother gave him. When he got to Jimmy's, waiting for him was his first fiddle. He thanked his cousin, carefully put the little fiddle in the sack and placed it gently over his back. Gingerly, he carried it home to show his mother and brothers his new treasure.

Nate quickly noticed that the fiddle was missing its first two strings. Joe did what he'd seen his older brothers and cousins do: he went to the tractor shed, grabbed the pliers and cut two wires from the shed's screen door. He stretched the wires and strung them on his new fiddle.

Soon, he taught himself his first song, "Hook and Line": "You get a line and I get a pole. Meet me at the crawdad hole." He knew the song well because he'd often heard his father play it. Joe took to playing the fiddle like a fish on his first swim. Within a week, he was ready to play for his family.

His first performance brought down the house. His mom was shocked. Nate thought Joe was awesome and let his little brother know it. John Arch was so impressed that the next day he started teaching Joe, who was a very fast learner. Soon after, John Arch finally took his precious fiddle down from the wall.

LITTLE JOE AND NATE PLAY FOR DANCES

At seven, Joe started going to dances with his father and brother Nate. Soon, they knew enough to play along with their father and uncles. Joe and Nate saw how seriously their elders took playing music. They soaked it all in. Soon, the little boys were playing their fiddle and banjo sitting on straight-backed chairs while their feet dangled above the floor.

Joe and Nate played more and more. Eventually, the little boys all but replaced their father and uncles as the musicians of choice at square dances and frolics. They learned to play for thirty minutes without stopping. Like their father and uncles, Joe and Nate were also wonderful singers. They'd sing the old songs, play their fiddle and banjo and take turns shouting out the square dance calls.

The music, singing, calling and dancing stirred the soul. The mood in the rooms was electric, and the dancing was feverish. Dancers were so locked into the flow of the music that they were barely conscious of their feet hitting the floor.

When not playing for dances, going to school or doing chores, Joe and Nate played at home every chance they got. Music was always on young Joe's mind. Years later, he recalled in the documentary about him:

> I'm going to tell you about playing music. I used to be out in the field working somewhere, maybe somewhere on the tractor…I had thought about a song I wanted to play. Well, that song come to me way out in the field…It didn't come to me while I had the fiddle in my hand. Then I come on to the house and picked it up and [went] to play it…It's got to be in you, you know. You've got to want to do it.

During the Depression, his father watched his brother Walter go into debt. When John Arch mortgaged his farm to try to help Walter, both of them ended up losing their farms to a white farmer. It was a huge blow to the family. Joe was around twelve years old. He always felt the farmer didn't give his father enough time to pay his debt. But Joe, his parents and his siblings were not ones to wallow in self-pity. John Arch went to work on the farm of their neighbor Joe Pittard.

Throughout the 1930s and into the early '40s, Joe and Nate stayed busy playing for local dances, both black and white. Joe and Nate sure knew how to drive a dance. They were experts on how to structure the rhythm, where to put the emphasis.

They continued to play the songs their father and uncles had taught them and also learned songs from other old-time musicians in the area. By the mid-1930s, these were mostly white musicians. After a day of working in the fields, Joe and Nate jammed with them on back porches.

By the 1930s, few blacks were playing old-time music. Most had moved away from it toward blues. Since the mid-1920s, the recording industry had been marketing "hillbilly" (old-time) music to whites and "race" (blues) music to blacks. In the mid-1930s, bluesman Blind Boy Fuller from nearby Durham was a popular recording artist.

Sometimes at the square dances, when the fiddlers and banjoists took breaks, Nate accompanied Cousin Odell on blues guitar. They played songs like Blind Boy Fuller's "Careless Love," and couples danced slow drags and the Charleston. Sometimes, the parties were straight blues dance parties. Joe did not get into the blues; he stuck exclusively to the old-time Thompson tradition.

In 1940, Joe was still living near Efland with his parents. He farmed for Claude Lynch. When he wasn't farming or fiddling for dances, he worked as an attendant at an Esso Service station near Mebane, in Alamance County, a town of around two thousand people about six miles away.

He must have been socializing, too, because in July 1942, at age twenty-three, he married Hallie Evans, two years his senior. Joe must have been on military leave at the time because his marriage took place six months after he enlisted at Fort Bragg as a private in the U.S. Army.

World War II Brings Changes to Joe's World

During World War II, Joe was a proud member of the Sixty-first Battalion out of Tampa, Florida, an all–African American engineering unit. The unit's job in Europe was to clear roads and build pontoon bridges bombed by the Germans. Joe drove a D7 armored bulldozer. On D-Day, June 6, 1944, Joe and his unit crossed the English Channel onto the beaches of Normandy.

When the war ended in 1945, Joe came home on Thanksgiving Day. The Burlington Police Department had contacted his father about a job for Joe. John Arch explained to Joe that it was a good job but that he would not be allowed to arrest white people. Joe turned the job down.

After World War II, Joe returned to a new world. The black frolics on farms had all but disappeared. Many rural blacks had jobs in nearby towns and cities. Some commuted; others moved to the cities. Most of them had left country life and customs behind. Radio stations oriented to blacks played blues, jazz and R&B, not old-time. Joe and Nate still played for a few dances, but by the late 1940s, square dancing was out of fashion for blacks and for many whites, too.

Proud and Happy in Mebane

In February 1946, Joe took a job at the White Furniture Factory. It was the biggest furniture maker in North Carolina and the largest employer in Mebane.

After serving in World War II, Joe wasn't willing to be treated like a second-class citizen at work. As he remembered in an interview with David Romtvedt years later:

> *They had a place that said: "Black folks don't drink here. White folks drink here." We tore that shit down that day…I wasn't going to put up with it. These things come up so simple sometimes. Clear enough for me.*

Joe would work at the White Furniture Factory for thirty-eight years. He would work as a ripsaw operator and a furniture finisher, loving his job and taking pride in his work.

Joe and his wife, Hallie, lived in a lovely home on a few acres in a rural part of Mebane, off Highway 119. It was only a few miles from the farm country where Joe grew up. Hallie was an insurance agent with the North

Carolina Mutual Life Insurance Company, the first black-owned insurance company in the United States. When Joe was not working at the White Furniture Factory, he tended his large garden and butchered his hogs in the fall. He was also busy as a father, as he and Hallie were raising Hassell McCoy Evans, their adopted son. In his free time, Joe served as a deacon at Kimes Chapel Missionary Baptist Church.

DETERMINED TO KEEP HIS FAMILY'S MUSIC ALIVE

For the most part, the world in which Joe and his siblings had grown up in rural Orange County was gone. Community frolics on farms had given way to evenings watching TV in air-conditioned rooms. Instead of wondering who would bring the pies to the dance after the corn shucking, families were watching their sons play Little League and daughters sell Girl Scout cookies.

By the mid-1950s, most blacks and whites had forgotten that African Americans had ever played old-time music. But the final blow to old-time music and the final insult for Joe was Elvis. Elvis took the nation by storm as millions flocked to his bluesy style of rock-and-roll. Some people even thought Elvis had invented this music style, when in fact, he was largely inspired by black music he'd heard growing up. In an interview with Joe Killian, Joe expressed his frustration: "Elvis Presley played the blues and took a lot of that music from black people. Then people thought that was white people's music, too. That messes black people up."

During the 1950s and '60s, Joe still played some old-time music. Joe's sister Effie's daughter, Dellaphine Ivey, remembered that Joe played the fiddle at his brothers' and sisters' houses at family gatherings. Dellaphine recalled the get-togethers as lively and fun. Banjo and fiddle music filled the air as older family members taught the younger ones to dance the old steps. Dellaphine remembered that on Friday nights, Joe also sometimes went out with Odell to play the occasional old-time dance.

Joe also played old-time music when he, his parents, his siblings and their kids visited Nate in Philadelphia. In the early 1950s, Nate had moved North for work. When his family visited, he'd take out his banjo and play the old songs with Joe, and Nate's neighbors in Philadelphia heard banjo and fiddle music.

But at the huge Thompson family reunions each year—which hundreds attended—no one brought a banjo or fiddle. Joe's second cousin Dr. Iris

Joe Thompson at home in Mebane, North Carolina, 2008. *Photo by David Persoff.*

Chapman—who produced the documentary on Joe—doesn't remember Joe or Odell playing at the reunions.

From time to time, Joe tried vainly to interest his adopted son and nieces and nephews in the fiddle or banjo. They were more interested in rhythm and blues and rock-and-roll. Joe was disappointed and frustrated that old-time music was meeting a dead end in the Thompson family line.

Though determined not to let his family's music die, Joe was becoming more and more of an oddity. When he went into music stores to ask about fiddles, salesmen were surprised. One such salesman was Clyde Davis at C.B. Ellis Music Co. in Burlington. In the 1960s, Davis wasn't used to seeing African American old-time fiddlers.

Cousin Odell also wanted to keep his family's music alive. Odell lived near Joe and was working in Mebane at a local mattress factory. In his spare time, he was visiting some local old-time jams. Old guys sat around together playing a mix of 1940s and '50s country, bluegrass and fiddle tunes. Soon, Odell bought a banjo and began playing clawhammer style, as his dad, Walter, had done decades before in Cedar Grove.

There were still some folks playing old-time music in North Carolina, but very few blacks. As seen in chapter two, young music pilgrims from around the country were discovering Tommy Jarrell and other musicians in Surry County. Academics like Alan Jabbour played in the Chapel Hill/Durham old-time scene. There were the fiddlers' conventions that attracted local old-timers and young hippies alike, such as the ones in Union Grove, North Carolina, and in nearby Galax, Virginia. But these people and events were not part of Joe and Odell's orbit—at least not yet.

THE FOLKLORISTS BEFRIEND JOE AND ODELL

That changed in 1973, when a Guilford College student from Upstate New York named Kip Lornell was traveling the back roads from Durham to Greensboro and stopped in Mebane. Since high school, Kip had been interviewing and doing field recordings of local black musicians, mostly acoustic blues players, first in Albany, New York, and now in the Piedmont of North Carolina. He was always on the lookout for interesting new subjects to interview and record, and since he was in no rush, he decided to take his chances on Mebane. He went into a store off Route 70 and asked a shopper if he knew of any blacks in the area who played blues guitar, banjo or fiddle.

The man told Kip that down the road lived a black banjo player named Odell Thompson. Kip went to Odell's house and introduced himself. At first, Odell didn't quite know what to make of the young college student, but he was pleased by Kip's interest and invited him in. Odell played his banjo and talked about growing up in northern Orange County surrounded by Thompson family music. The two hit it off, and Odell invited Kip back.

When Kip returned to Odell's place two weeks later, Joe was also there, with his fiddle. The cousins played for Kip, who was more than thrilled. The three became friends. During his two years at Guilford College and his year at UNC–Chapel Hill getting a master's in folklore, Kip often visited Joe and Odell. By that time, the cousins were the only active, black, old-time musicians in the Mebane area. Kip interviewed and recorded Joe and Odell. Sometimes, the cousins invited Kip to come along with them when they played for family members or, on rare occasions, neighbors.

Before leaving North Carolina to pursue further studies, Kip told other Chapel Hill folklorists and North Carolina folk music enthusiasts about the cousins. Over the next decade, Joe and Odell got a steady stream of visitors. Some of the young folklorists enjoyed jamming with the cousins. Cece Conway—who would become a professor at Appalachian State and author of *African Banjo Echoes in Appalachia*—was getting her PhD in Chapel Hill at the time. Working on a documentary about black banjoists and fiddlers, notably Dink Roberts, she was thrilled to meet the Thompsons. Others interested in Joe and Odell Thompson's music included Glenn Hinson, a future professor at UNC–Chapel Hill, and Wayne Martin, a future executive director of the North Carolina Arts Council.

Through the visits, the eager young folklorists let the cousins know their music was important and valued. They told Joe and Odell that more people would love to hear them play. At first, the cousins were skeptical that there was a public audience for their music. But the folklorists convinced them to give it a try. Before long, Joe and Odell were playing at colleges and music festivals around North Carolina. Instead of playing for farmers back in pre–World War II Orange County, Joe and Odell were playing for academics and hippies.

The timing was good for Joe and Odell. They were not only fine old-time musicians, but they were also African Americans with a family music pedigree that stretched back to the nineteenth century. This really grabbed the Chapel Hill scholars. After all, they were progressive young people who had just lived through the height of the civil rights movement. Joe liked to say that "the government" and the civil rights people had sent Kip Lornell to find him. Though the folklorists had studied the history of black old-time music, now they were befriending and playing music with the genuine articles. Like Joe, they'd been frustrated that most people—black and white—did not know that, for centuries, African Americans had played old-time music. Now, along with the cousins, they could open people's minds.

Joe was so moved by the folklorists' interest in him that he believed that playing the fiddle again in public was his divine purpose. He felt he was not only representing his family but his race, too. Joe tackled the challenge with the same seriousness he'd always applied to his music. He would make his family and his race proud.

And he did.

MAKING A HIT AT CARNEGIE HALL

Thanks to the scholars, Joe and Odell were now in the old-time network. They still had full-time jobs, but they performed whenever they could, mostly in North Carolina.

Audiences loved them. Before long, they were invited to play at the Festival of American Fiddle Tunes in Port Townsend, Washington, where they made a splash. Their success reinforced what Kip Lornell and others had been telling them: that people wanted to hear their music. Audiences found the music intense and exciting. Seeing and hearing African Americans play old-time was also eye-opening and refreshing. And the cousins were delightful entertainers.

Joe and Odell had different temperaments. Joe was a serious guy with a low-key sense of humor, while Odell was a charming, outgoing jokester. The two complemented each other well.

Onstage and off, Joe and Odell spoke of their fathers. In a 2012 WUNC radio interview with Frank Stasio, Wayne Martin remembered that Joe often said, "When you hear our music, you hear our fathers' music."

According to Martin, "Joe felt that he was carrying on something that he had been given, and he felt an obligation to share that." Joe thought of playing old-time music as what the Thompsons did, and he was intent on bringing his family's music to light.

In 1983, Joe retired from White Furniture and had more time to tour. Four years later, he lost his beloved Hallie. For years, she had been an invalid, and Joe had nursed her. Family and neighbors supported Joe in his grief. His young friends in the old-time network, which had grown in number over the past fifteen years, were also there for him. No longer working full time or needing to care for his wife, Joe had more time to tour with Odell.

In 1989, Joe turned down an offer to play at Carnegie Hall in New York City because he thought going to New York would be a hassle. But in 1990, he decided to go. Years later, in the documentary on his life, he recalled a conversation with his banker before leaving for New York:

Banker: What do you tell me you going to play next?
Joe: We got to go to New York.
Banker: New York?
Joe: Yeah.
Banker: Where at you all going to in New York?
Joe: Carnegie Hall.
Banker: Carnegie Hall?
Joe: Yeah, what's a matter with Carnegie Hall? (I didn't know about no Carnegie Hall or nothing. All I know is it's a hall like any other hall. That's what I was thinking. Well, I found out different.)
Banker: Joe, I don't think you quite know what you're running into now. Maybe I better lift you up here a little bit.
Joe: OK.
Banker: Carnegie Hall is the Big Apple…That's the world's best. I don't care where you go. Carnegie Hall is at the top…if you go well at Carnegie Hall and play and make a hit, you'll be a celebrity.

Joe and Odell were a hit at Carnegie Hall, complete with a two-minute ovation and a stellar review by the critic from the *New York Times*. It was a life-changing moment for the retired furniture factory worker. Joe's parents, who died in the 1960s, would have been immensely proud of their son. In an interview with Joe Killian of the *Greensboro News and Record*, Joe talked about his dad, "I wish my daddy could have seen me play Carnegie Hall…There are a lot of places I wish he could have seen me play, but at Carnegie Hall—you know you're important when you play there."

The gig at Carnegie Hall got Joe and Odell more recognition and work. In 1990, they won the Brown-Hudson Award from the North Carolina Folklore Society and, in 1991, the North Carolina Folk Heritage Award from the North Carolina Arts Council. They would go on to play around the country and overseas, including at the Kennedy Center, the Smithsonian Institution, the National Folk Festival and the International Music Festival in Brisbane, Australia.

LOSING ODELL

It was at MerleFest in 1994, at the height of the cousins' success, when life took a cruel turn. One night, Joe and Odell left their hotel and went across the street to the store. They started back together after they bought their food, but Odell turned back to get some toothpicks. Joe, unaware, had already begun crossing the street. Odell was trying to catch up with Joe when, out of nowhere, a car struck Odell and knocked him down. At eighty-three, he didn't survive.

Joe lost his cousin, musical partner and close friend. It was a harsh blow.

There to comfort Joe that night at the hospital was a banjoist who had been playing with the cousins at the festival: Bob Carlin. In 1975, Bob had come down from the New York City area to visit Tommy Jarrell as a friend of Ray Alden's. He'd fallen in love with the state and longed to return.

Bob Carlin was a fine banjoist and expert on all things banjo. In 1977, he moved to Philadelphia to take a job at WHYY hosting a folk music show. There, he heard from a folklorist friend that there was an African American banjo player living somewhere in the Philadelphia area.

In 1985, after nearly seven years of searching, Bob found Nate Thompson. Nate hadn't been playing much music at the time and told Bob to go see his brother Joe in North Carolina. On his periodic trips to North Carolina to do research and attend fiddlers' conventions, Bob had called Joe a number of times.

Bob finally met Joe. On one of his trips south, Bob attended his first Thompson jam session—riding over with Joe to Odell's house; sharing a meal cooked by Odell's wife, Susie; and then playing music with the cousins in the house and yard.

In 1989, Bob finally got the chance to move to North Carolina for good. He had taken a job as a visiting artist at Davidson County Community College. He presented Joe and Odell as part of his residency and had played with them from time to time since, which brought him to MerleFest that night.

Joe was beside himself. At the hospital that night, Joe had a lot of discussions with Bob. Joe kept asking, "Why did this happen to Odell? Should I keep playing?" In the documentary on him, Joe explained that he turned to God for answers:

I says to the Lord that night, well...why is all this here going on with me?...What is I'm going to have to tell the folks? You going to have to give me something to tell 'em. And He made it plain. He may not have spoke

*to me. I didn't hear no voice. But He said: "I had to separate you two."
That's what come in to my mind. And that thing followed me for a while:
"I had to separate you two." Because He didn't want me, then. He got the
one He was after.*

Joe's faith kept him going. It gave Joe strength, which helped him as he
grieved the loss of Odell in 1994 and then of Nate in 1997.

Joe's second cousin Iris Thompson Chapman felt Bob and others also
played a role. Helping Joe and performing with him were folks like Clyde
Davis, Alan Julich, Steve Terrill and Larry Vellani, to name a few. As Joe
explained in the documentary:

[Bob] *and so many other folks were willing to help me keep moving on.
Everybody wanted to help me play. Everybody was always ready. They just
kept me busy. A lot of time, I probably wouldn't have went, but they wanted
to go. So we just got started and so we never stopped going.*

With the help of his musician friends and the support of his second wife,
Pauline, Joe performed at festivals, summer camp workshops and schools.
He was a devoted teacher, very serious about passing along his family's music
to new generations.

TALKING TO THE MAN

In 2001, at age eighty-two, Joe had another setback: a major stroke. He
could hardly move his left hand. His doctor said that he'd never walk again
without a walker and never be able to tend his garden or play his fiddle.

But Joe's fierce independence wouldn't allow his doctor to have the last
word. Joe decided to "talk to the Man." Joe asked God whether He was
telling him to quit the fiddle. The answer came to Joe in subtle ways. At
the rehabilitation center, a neighbor held up Joe's hand while he played.
Memories of his father fiddling at frolics across northern Orange County
filled his mind.

Soon, Joe heard God's reply: a resounding "KEEP PLAYING." Before
long, using limited movement in his left hand, Joe was able to make his fiddle
sound as it had before the stroke. He was able to walk by himself and work
in his garden. As Bob Carlin said, "It was an amazing recovery."

INSPIRING THE CAROLINA CHOCOLATE DROPS

In 2005, Joe attended the Black Banjo Gathering at Appalachian State University in Boone. Organized by Professor Cece Conway, the event attracted musicians and historians from around the world. Attendees were thrilled to meet kindred spirits drawn to the same topic.

At the Gathering were three young musicians who, like Bob Carlin, Kip Lornell and Cece Conway, were fascinated by the history of old-time music. But these young musicians were different, too. They were a generation younger than Conway and company, and they were African American.

Rhiannon Giddens, Justin Robinson and Dom Flemons were immediately drawn to Joe. They loved not only his fiddling but also that he was the last surviving black old-time musician in North Carolina, if not in the nation. After the Gathering, Justin Robinson, who lived in the Durham area, started visiting Joe in Mebane. Soon, Dom Flemons followed, as did Rhiannon Giddens, who had met Joe once just before his stroke.

That summer, Dom, Rhiannon and Justin visited Joe every Thursday and jammed with him in his living room. Joe's Bible lay open on a table, and photos of his parents dotted the room. In between songs, Joe told his three eager students about the old days when he played with his father and brother at Orange County dances.

There were almost no other young African Americans learning old-time music—none in North Carolina—and Joe felt energized to be passing along his family's music to these terrific musicians. Joe, in his late eighties, thrived on the sessions, which lasted up to five hours. In an article in *Our State* magazine, Rhiannon recalled that "Joe never seemed to get tired as long as we were playing."

In the fall of 2005, Dom, Rhiannon and Justin formed a band called the Carolina Chocolate Drops. The band was a tribute to their mentor. They would sometimes bring Joe on stage with them, which audiences loved. When the group appeared at MerleFest with Joe, the audience went wild.

The Carolina Chocolate Drops are covered in more detail in chapter seven, but it's worth noting here that they went on to make a splash, performing around the country and the world. In 2010, they won a Grammy for their album *Genuine Negro Jig*. Joe was extremely proud.

Joe's protégés were also proud to carry forth their mentor's music. When Joe Thompson passed away in 2012, at age ninety-three, Dom Flemons felt a deep sense of loss and gratitude. Flemons paid this tribute to the master:

Joe Thompson with the Carolina Chocolate Drops, 2005, Mebane, North Carolina. *Left to right*: Rhiannon Giddens, Dom Flemons, Joe Thompson and Justin Robinson. *Photo by Lissa Gotwals.*

Joe Thompson changed my life. When I first met him in 2005, I had no idea that I would be so heavily involved in making music with him. One thing for sure is that...it has been a constantly humbling journey to be able to have said I worked with him...I am eternally grateful to you, Joe Thompson. May the Man have a solid place for you up yonder, because you've more than earned it.

LEGACY

Reacting to Joe's passing, Joe Newberry—one of Joe's frequent playing partners—told David Menconi of the *Charlotte Observer*:

Joe Thompson was a gentleman, and a gentle man...To hear his legacy in a younger generation of musicians is very satisfying to all of us who play this kind of music. He really was a one-of-a-kind fiddle player, and we're all lucky and honored to have just walked in his garden.

Joe Thompson never gave up. Against the odds, Joe fulfilled his mission to keep alive his family's music. More than seventy years after black old-time music had gone out of style, he continued to influence young musicians. Through the Carolina Chocolate Drops and others, Joe Thompson's music will inspire audiences around the world for years to come.

Some of Joe's Favorite Songs

"Corn Liquor"
"I Shall Not Be Moved"
"Molly Put the Kettle On"
"Oil in My Vessel"

Essential Joe Thompson CDs

Black Banjo Songsters of North Carolina and Virginia
Carolina Chocolate Drops and Joe Thompson
Joe Thompson: Family Tradition

Joe Thompson's Alamance County

Mebane Historical Museum, Joe Thompson kiosk

Joe Thompson Documentary

Steel Drivin' Man: The Life and Times of Joe Thompson (available at the Mebane Historical Museum)

4
DOC WATSON

COURAGE

At-a-Glance

---◆◆◆---

DATES: 1923–2012
INSTRUMENTS: Guitar, vocals, banjo
MUSIC STYLES: Old-time, bluegrass, folk, gospel and acoustic blues
HOME: Deep Gap, North Carolina
AWARDS: Eight Grammy Awards, National Medal of Arts, National
*   Heritage Fellowship, North Carolina Heritage Award*
LEGACY: Doc Watson is the best-known American folk guitarist in the world.
*   The "father of the flat pick guitar," he played at breakneck speeds and made*
*   it seem effortless. Best known for translating mountain fiddle tunes to guitar,*
*   Watson elevated the acoustic guitar from a rhythm to a lead instrument.*

HOME IN THE HILLS

Deep Gap is a remote settlement in the Blue Ridge Mountains east of
Boone. Near there, in 1923, Doc Watson was born Arthel Watson in a
wood cabin built on land that had been in his family since the 1790s.
Arthel's ancestors came to the North Carolina mountains from England,
Ireland and Scotland. The jigs, ballads and hymns they brought with them
across the Atlantic lifted their spirits as they tamed the wilderness.

Doc Watson, Blue Ridge Parkway, North Carolina, 1987. *Photo by Hugh Morton, [P081_NTBR2_003017] in the Hugh Morton Collection of Photographs and Films, the Wilson Library, University of North Carolina at Chapel Hill.*

The sixth of nine children, Arthel was welcomed into the world by his paternal grandmother, the local midwife. At birth, an infection destroyed his cornea, perhaps due to contaminated silver nitrate solution. Though as a boy he could perceive some light, he was blind for the rest of his life.

Arthel's father and neighbors built the small, wooden cabin where he was born. Three small bedrooms lodged the family: one for the parents, one for their three daughters and the third for their six sons. There was no electricity, telephone or running water. The floors had cracks wide enough to feed the chickens walking underneath. The walls, made of rough boards and pasted with paper and mud, failed to keep the cold out in winter. Often, the family awoke on pillows covered with frost.

Behind the cabin were the barn, garden and a field of corn. The farmland was poor, filled with hills, briars and small trees. A yoke of oxen plowed the field and pulled in the wood. Under the woodshed lay a cellar filled for the winter with fruits and vegetables from the garden and with sausage made from the family's three hogs. The nearest store was more than two miles away. Since the family did not own a vehicle, they walked.

Riches His Parents Gave Him

Arthel's mother, born Annie Greene (1895–1985), worked from sunrise to sunset. With the help of her daughters, she cooked, cleaned and canned food. She churned butter from milk from the family's two cows. In the garden, she raised almost everything her family ate, except sugar and coffee, which she bought from the store. Breakfast was typically cornbread and gravy. Biscuits were a costly treat because they required flour.

Throughout the day and evening, Annie Watson sang the old mountain ballads and hymns from the British Isles, which had been passed down in her family for centuries. She sang using a nasal tone unique to the Appalachian region, perhaps influenced by Cherokee singing styles. On a typical evening, she sang her children to sleep with mountain standards, such as "The House Carpenter" and "Omie Wise."

Arthel's father, General (1892–1949)—a given name, not a military rank—was a devoted family man and tireless worker. Son David remembered that one of his father's favorite sayings was: "Give a man a day's work for a day's pay." A day laborer, General worked on WPA construction jobs when they were available, helping build the Blue Ridge Parkway and Appalachian State University in Boone. Since he did not own a vehicle, he typically walked to the road at five o'clock in the morning or earlier to catch a ride to work from neighbors. His usual pay during the Depression was ten cents an hour. With the help of his sons, he also farmed his land, hunted for food and cut down trees from nearby hillsides. He sold the wood to local lumber companies and also used it for firewood at home.

Every Sunday, rain or shine, General and Annie Watson walked their large family three and a half miles to their small place of worship, Mount Paran Baptist Church. General was the leader of the church choir, and Arthel and his siblings regularly sang their father's favorite hymn, "The Lonesome Pilgrim." Joining in the singing were members of the extended Watson clan.

For Arthel's family, religion did not end on Sunday. Every evening of the week, General and Annie led the family in daily devotionals from the Bible, as well as in prayers and hymn singing from *The Christian Harmony* songbook. The family sat around the fireplace in a half circle, with Mom and Dad at the front surrounded by their nine children.

Annie and General Watson avoided community events where jugs of moonshine were passed around. This included barn raisings, quilt-making parties and square dances. Church communion was the one occasion liquor was allowed. Annie Watson made sacrament wine at home from her own grapes. When Arthel was about six, he discovered jars of fermenting wine under his parents' bed. A curious child, he unscrewed a lid, sampled the liquid and guzzled the sweet elixir. Before long, he was stumbling around the house. Watson cared little for liquor the rest of his life.

DEEP SIBLING TIES

Arthel's five brothers and three sisters were his best friends. Arthel had four older brothers—Arnold, Otis, Russeau and Linney—and an older sister, Ruby. He had three younger siblings: David, his constant companion, who was two years younger; Jewel, six years younger; and Ethel (also blind), eleven years younger. It was a close-knit, loving group. Neighbors liked to visit and enjoyed the harmony and laughter radiating from the Watson clan.

Arthel and David often joined their four older brothers to roam the countryside, fields and woods. The six brothers sledded down mountains, splashed in the creek, jumped on corncribs and climbed trees. General and Annie treated Arthel just like their sighted sons.

Sometimes Arthel's older brothers were hard on him, which required him to stand up for himself. One day, his older brothers built a sleigh out of a toolbox. The ground had frozen overnight, and the trip down the hill in the wooden sleigh was a very fast ride. Arthel really wanted to try it. His older brothers agreed to let him, promising they would catch him when he reached the bottom.

When Arthel arrived full speed at the bottom of the hill, his brothers broke their promise and only touched his arms instead of grabbing them. Arthel flew into a haystack. He knew his brothers had probably missed him on purpose and was livid. He kept playing with his brothers, though, and they stayed his close friends for life.

THE FIRST MUSIC HE LOVED

For the Watsons, music was as natural as breathing. It was part of daily life. Arthel and his siblings grew up surrounded by traditional Appalachian folk songs. On front porches and at community gatherings, they reveled in the old ballads, hymns and fiddle tunes.

Doc Watson in the Blue Ridge Mountains. *Drawing by Tracy Bigelow Grisman, 2015.*

Of all the siblings, Arthel was the most interested in all sorts of sounds. From an early age, he delighted in the sounds of trains and cowbells. As a little boy, Arthel banged on his mother's pots and pans to hear different tones. When his mother yelled at him that he was giving her a headache, he'd stop, but only for a while. He asked David to throw rocks by his head because he loved to hear the sound of them whirling by his ears. One day, one of these rocks hit him on the head.

Arthel's earliest memories of music were of sitting in his mother's lap as a toddler listening to his aunts, uncles, cousins and neighbors sing in the church choir. They sang the old a cappella hymns under the leadership of their choir director, General Watson. Many members of the congregation had great voices, and Arthel and his siblings soaked in what Arthel later remembered as "singing that was the greatest singing this side of heaven."

Every fall, for three or four days before the harvest, the Reverend Thomas Robbins taught a "singing school." Robbins was the grandfather of Arthel's future wife. He taught shape note singing out of *The Christian Harmony*, *The Southern Harmony* and *The Sacred Harp*. Singers crowded together in the small church and harmonized their best voices in joyous praise. Warm, vibrant tones flowed out of the open windows, lifting to the mountain sky.

When he was five or six, Arthel got his first instrument: a harmonica, a gift from his father. General taught Arthel how to play Appalachian folk songs, such as "Sally Gooden" and "Molly Hare." Arthel loved playing harmonica with his dad and his neighbor and cousin Spencer Miller. Arthel played the harmonica so much that none of his harmonicas lasted the year. But he was the only child who got a harmonica from his dad each Christmas.

TURNED ON TO RECORDS

In 1929, shortly after Arthel received his first harmonica, his parents bought a used Victrola. Arthel's father and brothers worked a few days at the local sawmill run by Uncle Jerome. At the end of the week, in exchange for their work, Uncle Jerome gave them his windup phonograph, which came with fifty 78rpm records. Arthel, his parents and his siblings loved sitting around the Victrola and listening to records that opened up a new world of music. They soaked in the popular songs of the day, including blues, Dixieland jazz and gospel tunes.

The Victrola's record collection included recordings by rural white performers, such as the Carter Family, Jimmy Rodgers, the Skillet Lickers, Uncle Dave Macon and the Smith Sacred Singers. The Watsons also listened to African American musicians, such as Mississippi John Hurt, Furry Lewis, Louis Armstrong and the Memphis Jug Band Stompers. Arthel and his family played the records so much that they wore them out.

HOMESICK AT BLIND SCHOOL

Because he was blind, Arthel was not able to attend the local, one-room school with his siblings. In 1933, when he was ten years old, his parents took advantage of the education the state provided for blind children. He would leave home and attend the Raleigh School for the Blind. Arthel boarded the bus alone and headed east two hundred miles.

Although often lonely and homesick at the school, Arthel was bright and received a fine education there. Good teachers brought him quickly up to grade level. One great perk was the school's excellent music department. Arthel took classical piano lessons for a while and even learned how to tune pianos.

Arthel's best friend at the school was Paul Montgomery, who remained his friend for life. Paul played guitar upside down and backward and taught Arthel some chords. Arthel and Paul liked many musical styles and felt constrained by the school's emphasis on classical music. Every chance they had, they listened to the radio and to country, big band and blues records.

Some of the children and many of the teachers at the school did not like the poor mountain kids. Sometimes, an especially mean teacher would knock Arthel's food to the floor and make him hunt for it and eat it. This upset him deeply. He was eager to return to Deep Gap as often as funds allowed. He would hop on the bus, head west, get off very late at night and fall into his family's loving arms.

Banging on a Homemade Banjo

The summer back home in Deep Gap after Arthel's first year at the Raleigh School for the Blind, he received a wonderful gift from his father: a homemade fretless banjo. General had carved the neck out of maple and the hoop out of hickory. Knowing Grandmother's sixteen-year-old cat was sick and on its last legs, General had convinced Linney to put the poor creature out of its misery. Its skin was thin and would give the banjo an excellent tone.

The first song General taught Arthel to play on his new banjo was "Rambling Hobo," followed by "Georgie Buck." Arthel's oldest brother, Arnold, also played the banjo and taught him some songs. Arthel loved playing the banjo. Here was an activity where his blindness had its advantages because it made him focus so deeply on sound. General was very pleased with his son's banjo playing. Years later, Watson recalled to radio host Terry Gross what his father had told him: "Son, I want you to learn how to play this thing real well. It might help you get through the world."

Arthel played his new instrument all the time, to the point that his parents sometimes hid it so they could have some quiet. When summer was ending and it was time to go back to school, Arthel brought his prized possession to Raleigh with him. Playing it lifted his spirits and made him feel less homesick.

Learning Chords on His First Guitar

In 1936, when Arthel was thirteen and home on vacation during his third year at the blind school, he received another surprise. One morning before going to work, General heard Arthel practicing chords he had learned from Paul Montgomery at school. Arthel was playing a guitar he'd borrowed from his cousin.

General made a deal with his son. If Arthel could play a complete song by the time he returned from work, he would help him buy his own guitar. By the end of the day, Arthel was strumming "When the Roses Bloom in Dixieland" by the Carter Family.

That Saturday, General took his son to a store in Wilkesboro to help him buy a twelve-dollar Stella guitar. Arthel paid for some of it from his savings, and General paid the rest with his hard-earned cash. From a mail-order catalogue, Arthel got the instruction booklet he needed. He was hungry to learn chords, and his brother David showed him where to place his fingers.

Country Music Radio's Golden Age

While home on another vacation that year, Arthel discovered his older brother Otis had bought a Crosley radio. Now, in addition to being able to play his banjo and guitar and listen to records, Arthel could explore an even wider world of music. This began many years of radio listening for Arthel and his family. Radio reception was often better at night, and they enjoyed not only local stations but also stations from as far away as Texas and Minnesota. During supper, the family listened to their favorite radio shows. On Saturday nights, they tuned into the *Grand Ole Opry*.

Arthel was lucky to be growing up when country music was exploding over the airways. Though he listened mostly to country, he also listened to blues and jazz, including big band and Dixieland. He soaked up the similarities and differences between musical styles.

He was enthralled by many of the country music performers of the day, especially Bill and Charlie Monroe, the Blue Sky Boys and J.E. Mainer's Mountaineers. He adored the guitar playing of the Delmore Brothers and their song "Deep River Blues." Arthel dreamed of one day playing like the country music stars he listened to on the radio.

Returning Home

Though things were getting more exciting in Deep Gap thanks to the radio, life in the seventh grade back at the Raleigh School for the Blind was getting worse. The meanness of some of the matrons was chipping away at his self-esteem. Treated like a misfit because of his blindness was bad enough, but being made to feel inferior because he was a low-income kid from the mountains added insult to injury. Life was growing unbearable.

One day, Arthel volunteered to perform in a school talent show. He proudly went on stage with his banjo and sang "I Like Mountain Music," "Cripple Creek" and other Appalachian tunes. After the show, one of the matrons in the boys' dormitory yelled at him that he was too vain and slapped his face. She was mad with him for playing "hillbilly" music, not classical. That was the last straw. Arthel left the school and refused to return.

The Power of a Crosscut Saw

Back in Deep Gap, fourteen-year-old Arthel was depressed. He sat at home and felt useless while his brothers and father worked outdoors all day. General soon realized his son badly needed something to do to help him feel better.

It was 1937, and Arthel's father and older brothers worked in the logging trade, then the biggest industry in the North Carolina mountains. The Watson men chopped down large trees and sold them to logging companies, while keeping some of the lumber to burn at home. But for Arthel, chopping down huge trees was too risky.

General had a safer job in mind: working a crosscut saw, a task that would keep Arthel out of the way of falling trees. Arthel held the handle on one end of the saw while his father held the other. With the blade in between them, they cut into the lumber from the huge trees their brothers had chopped down. It was tiring work that used most of their muscles, but what a sense of achievement for Arthel. Realizing he could help his father and family, he beamed with pride.

Learning to work a crosscut saw gave Arthel the confidence he needed to think of himself as a useful person. He didn't have to sit in a corner because of his handicap. Years later, in the Terry Gross interview, he recounted that life-changing event: "That one thing, [my father] putting me to work,

Doc Watson, Deep Gap, North Carolina, 1964. *Photo by Dan Seeger, [Pf-20001/1905_01] in the John Edwards Memorial Foundation Records, Southern Folklife Collection, the Wilson Library, University of North Carolina at Chapel Hill.*

realizing I was worth something, might have been the thing that gave me the nerve to tackle music as a profession and get out there and face the world."

For the next two years, Arthel continued to build confidence. In addition to chopping wood, he helped his mother around the house and continued his learning by listening to books on tape.

He spent the rest of his free time playing music, either alone or with family and neighbors. He often played three or four hours a day. He loved to sit on the porch swing of his mountain home and play his banjo and guitar.

Two Fingers and a Flat Pick

By age sixteen, Arthel had begun busking weekends on the streets of Boone and Lenoir, sometimes with his older brother Linney. In Boone, Arthel played his guitar and banjo for tips at fruit stands, taxi stands and in front of Wilson's Barber Shop. In Lenoir, he often played at the Hog Waller marketplace. Some of what he played were the old mountain songs he learned from older relatives and neighbors. But most of his repertoire was contemporary songs on records and radio. "Weeping Willow" by the Carter Family was an audience favorite. Arthel became known as an excellent singer and guitar picker. Between songs, he delighted listeners with good-natured jokes and folktales.

In 1940, when Arthel was seventeen, he decided it was time to upgrade his Stella guitar. A chance arose for him and David to make some money. Many diseased chestnut trees had died and fallen in the area. Arthel and David cut up many of the trees and sold the wood to a dealer in Wilkesboro. With the money he earned, Arthel bought a Silvertone guitar from the Sears Roebuck catalogue. He also bought a Nick Lucas guitar instruction book and a flat pick.

Though Arthel had been playing the guitar since thirteen, he focused on practicing special techniques on his new Silvertone. On the radio, he started listening more closely to the techniques of the Delmore Brothers and to his new favorite, Merle Travis. Listening to Travis's guitar technique, Arthel made a discovery that inspired his own self-taught two-finger style. Using his thumb and index finger, he could play the lead, chords and melody at the same time. He felt excited that he could play "Deep River Blues" solo and make it sound like it did when the two Delmore brothers performed it on the radio.

Now that he had a pick, he changed his sound again. Arthel went back to his 78rpm records and focused on the guitar runs. Listening intently, he realized Jimmy Rodgers was playing with a flat pick. Using a pick, Arthel began to teach himself the same style. He decided he could also use a pick to make the Carter Family songs he'd been playing sound better.

All his experimenting and practicing was paying off. Arthel began winning prizes at contests and fiddlers' conventions. Adept at using his two-finger and flat pick playing techniques, he was making a name for himself as one of the area's best young guitar players.

"Call Him 'Doc'!"

Arthel was eighteen in 1941 when he got his nickname. One day, he was playing in a band at a furniture store in Lenoir, with the show being broadcast on radio station WHKY out of nearby Hickory. The radio announcer asked Watson his name. When he replied, "Arthel," the announcer asked if anyone in the audience could think of a catchier name for radio. A girl in the back of the audience shouted out, "Call him 'Doc'!" and the name stuck. It became not only his radio name but his everyday name, too.

During Doc's late teens, he sometimes teamed up with older musician Clarence Ashley to make a few extra dollars playing land sales. Ashley was a ballad singer and banjoist who, in the 1920s, had made records with the Carolina Tar Heels. Ashley had also performed as part of a traveling medicine show. When the auctioneer took his break, Ashley and Doc played wonderful old mountain songs.

Rosa Lee Captures His Heart

Around this time, in the early 1940s, Doc enjoyed going across the mountain a few miles from his parents' home to play fiddle tunes with one of the area's best old-time fiddlers, Gaither Carlton. One day, when Doc went to the Carlton home to visit and play music, also there were Gaither's wife and daughters, seven-year-old Irene and nine-year-old Rosa Lee. Doc loved hearing them sing. When Doc returned about a year later and Rosa Lee was there, he again noticed her beautiful voice.

In 1944, the Carltons moved across the mountain to a house nearer to the Watsons. Rosa Lee, then around fourteen, was unpacking dishes when Doc came over to visit. When Rosa Lee said hello, he felt like he had been hit on the head with a brick. Despite the almost nine-year age difference, he was in love.

Doc and Rosa Lee began to spend more time together, and Doc taught Rosa Lee guitar. During their courtship, his favorite song to play for her was "Shady Grove." Rosa Lee loved to hear Doc's nimble fingers plucking the song's minor notes and his soothing, baritone voice.

CLOSE-KNIT FOURSOME

In 1947, Doc and Rosa Lee married. He was twenty-three and she fifteen. The young couple moved in with Doc's parents, and in 1949, they had their first child. They named him Eddy Merle Watson after two of Doc's favorite country music stars, Merle Travis and Eddy Arnold. Everyone called the baby Merle. The family of three soon moved to a rental house nearby with electricity. In 1951, daughter Nancy was born.

Doc, Rosa Lee, Merle and Nancy were a happy and close-knit family. They enjoyed simple times together—singing songs, listening to the radio, sitting around their picnic table in the warm weather and reading the Bible in the evenings. In 1953, Doc and Rosa Lee scraped together what little money they'd saved and bought a small house nearby.

Doc received money from a few sources: the North Carolina Aid for the Blind, busking, piano tuning and occasional odd jobs. Around the house, he chopped wood and did more home repairs than many sighted husbands. Money was tight, and material possessions were few. The family was happy, though, rich in love and the solid, steadfast values of their mountain relatives and neighbors.

FIDDLE TUNES ON ELECTRIC GUITAR

Doc's music continued to play a major role in his life. He played a lot around the house and on the streets. But being blind blocked him from getting the amount of work he deserved. Many musicians didn't want him in their bands because he could not dance around on stage and perform in a flashy manner, a performance style typical of the day. His family's love and support helped relieve some of his frustration.

In 1952, Doc's mood and his musical prospects improved when he purchased an electric guitar and met a local musician and railroad worker named Jack Williams. Williams recognized Doc's virtuoso talent and wanted to give the handicapped musician the break he deserved. The two hit it off, and they formed a country dance band with Doc on vocals and lead electric guitar. The band, Jack Williams and the Country Gentlemen, played Friday and Saturday night dances at Lions clubs and Elks lodges. The band delighted audiences with its country, rockabilly and swing music and its square dance fiddle tunes.

Most of the time, the band didn't have a fiddler, so Doc taught himself to play lead fiddle on his electric guitar. He played complex fiddle songs, such as "Beaumont Rag," at a breakneck pace. Doc did not invent this technique out of thin air—he had heard Grady Martin and Hank Garland do something similar on records in the 1940s—but he refined and perfected it. Saturday night audiences were thrilled. Playing mountain fiddle tunes on acoustic guitar would one day become the technique for which Doc was best known. Over the years, many guitarists tried to imitate his amazing skill, but none could match it.

Doc Meets Ralph Rinzler

In the late 1950s, while Doc was in his mid-thirties and still playing electric guitar at dances with Jack Williams and the Country Gentlemen, a commercial boom exploded around the country called the "folk revival." The growing audience for folk music nationwide included many college-educated, urban and suburban young people.

Prior to the commercial folk explosion, folk music on college campuses and in urban areas outside the South was largely underground. These folk enthusiasts were not interested in commercial music; they were searching for old folk songs in scholarly books and on arcane records. The most influential of these records was a multi-disc set of southern folk songs from the 1920s and '30s edited by Harry Smith. Released in 1952 by Folkways Records, it was called the *Anthology of American Folk Music*.

One such enthusiast searching for authentic folk music was Ralph Rinzler, who grew up in Passaic, New Jersey, near New York City. A member of the folk singing club at Swarthmore College near Philadelphia in the mid-1950s, Rinzler was inspired when he heard Pete Seeger sing and play his banjo at the school. After Swarthmore, Rinzler befriended Pete Seeger's half brother Mike Seeger, and together with John Cohen they formed a bluegrass group: the Greenbriar Boys.

At a music festival in Maryland, Rinzler, Seeger and Cohen became enthralled by the music of Bill Monroe and the Stanley Brothers. To them, Monroe and the Stanleys sounded similar to the music they'd heard on the *Anthology of American Folk Music*. They realized southern old-time musicians were still performing and were not just a thing of the past heard on old recordings. Believing there was an audience up North for southern old-time musicians, Rinzler and his friends decided to head south on a discovery mission.

Doc Watson at the North Carolina Folk Heritage Awards, Raleigh, North Carolina, 1994. *Photo by Alan Westmoreland, from the General Negative Collection, courtesy of the State Archives of North Carolina.*

One reason that Rinzler and friends believed that there was an audience for southern old-time musicians was that pop culture had discovered folk music. The most significant event that launched the burst of fascination with folk music was the 1958 release of a watered-down version of the ballad from Wilkes County "Tom Dooley." The performers were a group of middle-class college kids from Hawaii and California called the Kingston Trio. Their version of "Tom Dooley" made it to number one on the *Billboard* pop chart.

RINZLER STRIKES GOLD AT UNION GROVE

In 1960, the Greenbriar Boys drove to Union Grove, North Carolina, to compete in the venerable fiddlers' convention and see if they could find some of the old-timers from the *Anthology of American Folk Music*. When Rinzler met Clarence Ashley, a ballad singer who performed on the collection, he knew he'd struck gold.

Six months later, Rinzler returned to North Carolina to record Ashley and his band. Ashley brought along a musician friend whom Rinzler had not met, Doc Watson. When Doc showed up for the session with his electric guitar, Rinzler thought he was strictly an electric rockabilly musician and wanted no part of him. Rinzler knew the folk audiences up North liked authentic, acoustic music, and anything electric would turn them off.

Doc refused to give up his electric guitar. Local audiences loved his electric guitar playing. The idea seemed absurd that people in urban areas and college campuses up North had an interest in the old-time music of his parents and grandparents. Old-time music had become an embarrassment to most young people living around Boone at the time. They preferred the more modern, popular music styles.

But on the way to the session, something happened that changed both men's lives. Doc, Clarence Ashley and musicians Clint Howard and Fred Price were sitting in the front cab of the truck. Rinzler was in the back playing his banjo. Suddenly, the truck stopped, and Doc jumped out of out of the cab and into the back with Rinzler.

Doc asked to borrow Rinzler's banjo and proceeded to play "Tom Dooley" in a more authentic style than the Kingston Trio's version. Doc told Rinzler he knew a lot of other old-time songs and that his family had been playing them in the mountains for generations. A century earlier, his great-grandmother had known Tom Dooley and his ill-fated sweetheart, Laura Foster.

Rinzler was floored. Doc not only was the genuine article but also a great musician. Rinzler felt more determined than ever to convince Doc to play acoustic guitar at the recording session. By the end of the drive, Doc was willing to put aside his doubt and believe the old songs of his parents and grandparents were of interest to young people up North. He played acoustic guitar at the session. *Old-Time Music at Clarence Ashley's* has remained a classic for over half a century.

ON THE LONESOME ROAD

Months later, Doc, Clarence Ashley, Fred Price, Clint Howard and Doc's father-in-law, Gaither Carlton, drove to New York City to play at the Friends of Old Time Music concert. Rinzler organized the concert at a public school in Greenwich Village. The audience loved them. Rinzler then booked the group three thousand miles away at the Ash Grove in Los

Angeles. He drove the musicians across the country, minus Gaither, who decided to stay home in Deep Gap. An eager audience awaited the North Carolinians on the West Coast.

At first, many folk fans came to see Clarence Ashley, whom they knew from the *Anthology of American Folk Music*. But soon, Doc Watson was the most popular of the group. People were impressed by his virtuoso guitar playing and rich baritone voice. His delivery of the old songs was smoother and less twangy than the other musicians. They also loved his down-to-earth personality and down-home stories. This mixture of qualities was exactly what folk revival audiences craved. Doc was a window into a different culture, and he drew urban listeners into his world in a wonderful way.

In 1962, at Gerdes Folk City in Greenwich Village, Doc's first solo performance was a big success. By 1963, Rinzler had convinced Doc to go solo full time. The next year, Doc was touring the United States as a solo artist, playing in concert halls and at colleges, festivals and hootenannies. For his New York appearances, Doc typically took the bus from Boone; transferred in Bristol, Tennessee; and then took the express bus to Manhattan. Once there, he was dependent on Rinzler or someone connected to the show venue to meet him. It was a long and difficult trip.

Being on the road away from Rosa Lee, Nancy and Merle was lonesome. Doc was limited in terms of what he could do during the day. He listened to books on tape, played the guitar and socialized with venue owners who let him stay in their homes. When in New York, he stayed with Rinzler, who managed his career. But more times than he would have liked, he stayed in cheap motel rooms. What made the hard work, monotony and loneliness of the road bearable was playing for audiences who loved the old, authentic songs from his mountain home.

In 1963, the prospect of a stay in a Philadelphia fleabag almost ended Doc's solo career. He had a two-week gig at the Second Fret downtown and paying for a hotel room across the street would have eaten up most of his earnings. A young African American cook at the club, Jerry Ricks, saw Doc's distress and offered him a room in his house. Doc chipped in with the groceries and played music with his host, who was a fine blues musician. Thanks to Ricks's kindness, Doc cleared $200 from the gig and decided to continue touring. What kept him going was the knowledge that he was making a living for his family.

Later that year, from his earnings from touring, Doc was able to get off Aid to the Blind. He wrote a letter to Raleigh explaining that he did not need

Doc Watson with David Holt, North Carolina Museum of Art, Raleigh, North Carolina, 2007. *Photo by FlyingRooster Photography, courtesy of David Holt.*

the aid anymore, and he paid his first income tax. His family, especially his twelve-year-old daughter, Nancy, was very proud.

When not on the road, Doc loved being home in Deep Gap. His handiness around the house was amazing. He rewired his house for electricity, built a utility shed and climbed on the roof to make repairs. With Merle, he cut down trees and chopped them for wood. He also loved to relax and listen to records or catch up with family and friends. Deep Gap was the place he loved best.

MERLE HELPS HIS DAD

One day in 1964, when he returned home from a tour, Doc received a big surprise. Rosa Lee had taught fifteen-year-old Merle some guitar chords. Merle was an incredibly fast learner. He had Doc's natural musical talent.

In 1965, Merle joined Doc on the road. Doc considered Merle his best friend, musical partner and guide. They typically did three hundred shows a year. For over fifteen years, father and son performed around the country and the world, including Japan, Europe and Africa.

Merle encouraged his father to add different music styles to his repertoire. Doc had already done this to some extent and was eager to do more, as he loved all kinds of music. In 1972, Doc participated on the groundbreaking album *Will the Circle Be Unbroken*, produced by the California folk-rock group the Nitty Gritty Dirt Band. This project expanded the Watsons' audience after the folk revival ended.

Merle formed the band Frosty Morn. He, Doc and bandmates T. Michael Coleman, Joe Smothers and Bob Hill mixed old-time and bluegrass songs with more modern music. They played tunes by artists such as Bob Dylan and the Moody Blues. After the band disbanded, T. Michael Coleman, bass player and harmony singer, continued to tour with Merle and Doc. The three kept exploring new musical directions.

In 1985, Merle died at age thirty-six in a tractor accident. Doc was devastated. Shortly afterward, Doc had a dream in which Merle encouraged him to continue to tour. Doc pulled together all his strength and decided to press on.

Jack Lawrence accompanied him for over a decade. Beginning in 1991, Merle's son Richard, a fine blues guitarist, started performing with his grandfather. From 1998 until Doc's passing in 2012, David Holt accompanied Doc. Holt encouraged Doc to dig out some of his older songs and tell his life stories on stage. In 2002, Watson and Holt's three-CD set based on their concerts—*Legacy*—won a Grammy Award for Best Traditional Folk Album.

From shortly after Merle's death until his own passing in 2012, a continual focus for Doc was MerleFest, the music festival he and Rosa Lee began in 1988 in memory of their son. In its first year, MerleFest attracted a few thousand music lovers to Wilkes Community College in Wilkesboro, not far from Deep Gap. Festival attendance has risen to about eighty thousand people of all ages. MerleFest is one of the largest and most popular music festivals in the United States. Attendees flock to it from all over North Carolina, the country and the world. MerleFest bills itself as "traditional plus," and festivalgoers enjoy bluegrass, as well as blues, zydeco, jazz, rock and more. Doc performed center stage at the festival each year, including in 2012, just one month before he died.

A LEGACY OF LOVE

Doc Watson's spirit lives on in the hearts of the millions of people who love him and his music. Fans adore him not only because he was a one-of-a-kind musician but also because he was a humble, honest and courageous person.

Watson overcame the challenges of blindness and poverty to become a music legend loved around the globe. His humility, bravery and perseverance were a testament to his upbringing in the North Carolina mountains and the lifetime he lived there with his parents, siblings, wife, children, cousins and neighbors. All of them were enriched to have loved him, the boy born blind on rugged soil who became one of the world's most famous troubadours.

Doc Watson had a deep impact on millions of people. His biggest influence, however, was on the people who knew him best. According to Kermit Watson, Doc's nephew, "Doc leaves a legacy of love."

According to David Watson, Doc's younger brother, "Doc will be remembered as being down-to-earth…people loved him for being that way."

For David Holt, Doc's close friend and musical partner, "Doc will be remembered as one of America's best folk musicians; there's nobody better. He carried older traditions forward and made them something people still cared about."

In 2002, on the *Legacy* CD, Holt asked Doc how he wanted to be remembered. Doc replied:

> *As a good old down-to-earth boy who didn't think he was perfect and who loved music. I'd like to leave quite a few friends behind, and I hope I will. Other than that, I hope nobody will put me on a pedestal when I leave here. I'm just one of the people, just me.*

Inscribed on the plaque of Doc Watson's statue in downtown Boone are the words he requested: "JUST ONE OF THE PEOPLE."

Essential Doc Watson CDs

Ballads from Deep Gap
Doc Watson
Doc Watson and Son
Doc Watson on Stage

Essential Doc Watson
Legacy: Doc Watson and David Holt
Milestones: Legends of the Doc Watson Clan (book/4-CD set)

Favorite Doc Watson Songs

David Holt's favorite: "John Henry"
Doc's favorite, according to Kermit and David Watson and David Holt: "Shady Grove"
Other favorites included "Deep River Blues" and "Ready for the Times to Get Better"

Doc Watson's Deep Gap Region

Doc Watson statue (downtown Boone)
MerleFest (Wilkesboro)
MusicFest 'n Sugar Grove: The festival bills Doc and Rosa Lee's name above the title as appreciation for their years of support for the event.
Todd General Store: For many years, Doc headlined an annual fundraiser at the nearby park in Todd to raise money for community projects.
Union Grove Old Time Fiddlers' Convention
Wilkes Community College, Eddy Merle Watson Garden of the Senses (Wilkesboro)

Doc Watson Documentary

Doc & Merle

MerleFest Website

MerleFest.com

EARL SCRUGGS

LOCAL ROOTS OF THE BANJO MASTER

At-a-Glance

---◆◆◆---

DATES: 1924–2012
INSTRUMENTS: Banjo, guitar, vocals
MUSIC STYLES: Bluegrass and beyond
HOME: Shelby, North Carolina
AWARDS: Five Grammy Awards, National Heritage Fellowship, National Medal of Arts, International Bluegrass Hall of Honor Inaugural Inductee, Country Music Hall of Fame member, star on Hollywood Walk of Fame
LEGACY: Earl Scruggs was to the banjo what Babe Ruth was to the baseball bat. Rarely, if ever, has an American musician so single-handedly brought an instrument into the mainstream and inspired so many others to play it. For over half a century, Earl Scruggs's three-finger technique has literally defined bluegrass banjo playing. The standard style used in bluegrass is called "Scruggs style."

THE SHY BOY FROM FLINT HILL

Earl Eugene Scruggs was born in 1924 in Cleveland County, North Carolina, fifty miles west of Charlotte. The county lay on the western boundary of the

Earl Scruggs at WHKY, Hickory, North Carolina, circa 1947. *Photo courtesy of the North Carolina Museum of History/Jim Mills Collection.*

North Carolina Piedmont. Earl grew up in a community called Flint Hill, about nine miles southwest of Shelby, the county seat. Flint Hill had a church, a tiny grade school and fewer houses than could be counted on one hand.

Just east of the Appalachians, the area's often-foggy landscape was filled with lush green hills and pine forests, dusty roads and cotton fields. It was also home to many textile mills.

For many generations, in Cleveland County and adjoining Rutherford County, the Scruggs family had been farmers. Earl, his parents and his siblings lived in a small wood-frame house on forty acres. The family survived by working their land. Cotton was their cash crop; to eat, they grew corn, wheat, beans, potatoes and okra. They plowed the fields with the help of their mule, Old Maude. The Scruggses were down-to-earth, church-going folk who worked hard each day to get by.

MUSICALITY OF THE SCRUGGS FAMILY

Both of Earl's parents were musical. Earl's father, George Elam Scruggs (1876–1928), was a respected farmer and bookkeeper. He was also a fine musician who played the fiddle and clawhammer banjo.

Earl's mother, Georgia Lula Ruppe (1892–1955), was sixteen years younger than her husband. Lula was a strong, religious woman devoted to her brood. In addition to taking care of her family and farm, she played the pump organ at church.

Earl—a shy, quiet and smart child—had two older brothers and three older sisters. Eula Mae was eleven years older than Earl, and Ruby Mae was four years older. Junie, Earl's oldest brother, was twelve years older. Horace, Earl's closest sibling in age, was almost two years older. All of Earl's older siblings played the guitar and banjo.

On banjo, Earl was following in his brother Junie's footsteps. At an early age, Earl also picked up his brother Horace's main instrument, the guitar. Earl and his siblings sometimes played a fiddle and an autoharp that were lying around the house. Earl mostly played banjo and guitar. But right from the start, the instrument that grabbed him the most was the banjo.

In the 1920s, when Earl was a boy, the banjo was hugely popular. And in Cleveland County, the banjo was really big. In his instruction book, *Earl Scruggs and the 5-String Banjo*, Scruggs wrote:

> *I grew up in the southwestern Piedmont section of North Carolina, and for some reason that region was a hotbed for 5-string banjo pickers. I've never heard of any other place in the world at that time where so many banjo players were picking two- and sometimes three-finger styles like they were in that one remote area of the United States.*

EARL'S MUSICAL MODEL: SMITH HAMMETT

In the area where Earl grew up, Smith Hammett (1887–1930) was the best and most influential three-finger banjo picker. Earl always thought Hammett was also the first in the area to play in that three-finger style. Hammett was married to Essie Ola Harris, a cousin of Earl's mother. The families got together often to enjoy each other's company and play music.

When Earl was growing up, most of the banjo pickers around him played in a style similar to Hammett's. They picked up on the strings with two or three fingers. Since the 1890s, using fingers to up-pick the strings had been popular in the Piedmont. Earl's father was one of the few banjoists who still played the old African-derived, down-stroking clawhammer style.

Charlie Poole (1892–1931) probably did not directly influence Smith Hammett or other three-finger pioneers in the region where Earl grew up. The Shelby-area pickers played old instrumentals, while Poole sang most of his repertoire, much of which came from Tin Pan Alley and other popular sources. Also, according to bluegrass banjoist and historian Jim Mills, Charlie Poole's playing mechanics were different from the Shelby-area pickers. Likely, the three-finger style that Smith Hammett and others played—the style that would greatly influence Earl Scruggs—was largely regional.

Smith Hammett was born near Gaffney, South Carolina, less than twenty miles south of Shelby. He was from a musical family and played multiple instruments from a young age. His favorite from the start was the banjo.

In 1920, Hammett arrived a crackerjack banjo player when he began work in the Cliffside Cotton Mill, about fifteen miles southwest of Shelby. Working in the mill, Hammett mined its rich musical talent. He formed bands with co-workers, who played music on breaks, after work and on weekends. A band led by Smith Hammett was a standout at local fiddlers' conventions and square dances. Hammett and bandmates took infectious fiddle standards like "Cripple Creek" and "Cumberland Gap" and adapted them to a three-finger style.

By the mid-1920s, the Hammett and Scruggs families often spent time in each other's homes. At the end of each visit, they played music. Years later, in an interview with Don Borshelt, Earl's older brother Junie recalled Smith Hammett's banjo playing: "Smith had come by our house from a dance, and Mom and Dad fixed him a snack. He started playing the banjo. I woke up and thought that was the prettiest music I ever heard."

Listening to Hammett's fine three-finger banjo picking inspired Junie to take up the banjo. In 1927, when Junie was about sixteen years old, he ordered one from a mail-order catalogue for the lofty sum of seventeen dollars. Every chance he could, he played it, using the three-finger style. Earl was three at the time and soaking it all in.

When Earl played Junie's adult banjo or his father's three-dollar one, the rim was too big for his lap. He had to rest the banjo to his right. Sometimes, as he tried to reach different places on the neck with his left hand, he accidentally slid the banjo's head around. This scratched the rim, and Junie got mad.

Smith Hammett took a special interest in Earl and let him play a mini-banjo he owned. Its head was only nine inches in diameter, and the neck was shortened. The banjo fit Earl perfectly and made him feel like a grownup.

Hammett would play a banjo game with Earl. He'd play a tune, and Earl would try to copy him. Locals gathered around to listen. Earl was gaining a reputation as a child prodigy.

When Earl taught himself to play the banjo beginning at age four, he played with his thumb and index finger. He had an idea of what he wanted to hear, and he knew that using three fingers like Junie and Smith Hammett would make the banjo sound fuller, richer and more flowing. But picking with two fingers would do for now. More than anything else, Earl loved playing the banjo, and he dreamed of being a famous banjoist one day.

MOURNING AT THE SCRUGGS HOME

In 1928, when Earl was still four years old, he and his family suffered a major blow. After an eight-month fight with cancer, George Elam Scruggs died. Earl was left without a father and with a hole in his heart. Years later, in his instruction book, Earl explained, "I remember him, but not very well. I remember when he was sick. It really used to bother me growing up an awful lot."

Immersing himself in the banjo was Earl's way of honoring his dad's memory and dealing with his loss. Playing his father's old banjo kept Earl company and made him feel better. He knew it had done the same for his dad. Through the banjo, Earl felt connected to the father he loved dearly but had barely known.

Two years later, in 1930, at the start of the Great Depression, six-year-old Earl suffered another blow. At forty-two years of age, Smith Hammett was killed in a violent fight. It was a sudden loss and another premature one.

Hammett's funeral drew one of the largest crowds that had ever been at his church. One of the pallbearers was eighteen-year-old Junie Scruggs.

Smith Hammett had wanted to give Earl his mini-banjo as a gift, but that was not to be. What Smith Hammett and George Scruggs left behind for Earl was their priceless passion for the banjo.

CONSTANT HOMEMADE MUSIC

When Earl was a young boy growing up fatherless at the onset of the Depression, his family couldn't afford a radio and didn't go to the movies. Homemade music was their entertainment.

On Sunday afternoons after church, Earl and his older siblings got out the banjo, guitar and fiddle and played for hours. They played sacred songs and old-time mountain classics like "Sally Goodin" and "Cripple Creek." They learned a lot of songs from neighbors and relatives, many of whom were fine front porch pickers.

The Scruggs kids also played songs they learned from listening to records on their wind-up gramophone. Earl loved their two Jimmie Rodgers records that came with the machine. Earl listened intently to their Carter Family records and tried to copy Maybelle Carter's guitar playing. The Scruggses also owned several pop records with a horn band. Earl liked them and learned to play a peppy, big band number named "Farewell Blues."

Earl and his siblings also enjoyed music at family reunions and gatherings. Relatives danced, surrounded by toe tapping and smiling faces. This relaxed music-making and dancing offered the family an escape from hard times.

The Scruggses went to a Baptist church in the country. All day long on special days, friends and neighbors would gather on the church lawn and sing the old hymns. The songs that congregants belted out into the Cleveland County air lifted their spirits and calmed their nerves. Singing their hearts out to Jesus helped the hardscrabble folk of Flint Hill forget their worldly concerns. Singing was followed by "dinner on the grounds," a delicious spread of homemade southern favorites. Earl and the others feasted and soaked in the fellowship and singing as the daylight faded and stars covered the Piedmont sky.

PLAYING IN PUBLIC AT AGE SIX

When Earl was six, he first played in public. He made his debut at a fiddlers' convention a couple miles away in Boiling Springs. Earl walked down a dusty, dirt road to the event picking his banjo. Once there, he played "Cripple Creek" for the judges. They were impressed by his focus and picking and awarded him a top prize.

During the same year, one or two nights a week, Junie played his banjo for square dances. At one of the dances, on back-up rhythm guitar, was his little brother Earl. Since Junie liked to play banjo, Earl played guitar.

Later in 1930, Junie took his brothers Horace and Earl 140 miles to Spartanburg, South Carolina, where the three performed on a 7:00 a.m. radio show on WSPA. The brothers were ages six, eight and seventeen. All over the South, country music radio shows were popping up on the airwaves, but not many of them featured six-year-olds.

A UNIQUE WAY TO PRACTICE TIMING

Earl lived in a banjo-centric world. The sounds of the banjo were always running through his mind. When he wasn't playing the banjo, he thought about it—at school, playing games with friends and doing chores around the house and farm. Later, he wrote in his book that he was "living and breathing the banjo."

In winter, Earl built fires in the cookstove so his mother could make breakfast. Then, while the stove heated up, he took out his banjo and played. Lula Scruggs prepared a hearty first meal of the day. Her son's mouth watered while the room filled with the aroma of cornbread and the sounds of an old-time banjo tune.

When they finished their farm chores, and on winter evenings after homework, Earl practiced with Horace. The two would stand back to back on the porch. With Horace playing the tune on guitar and Earl on banjo, they would walk around the house in opposite directions.

Their goal was to meet up on the other side of the house playing the song in perfect time. If they weren't in unison, they would walk to the front of the house and do it again until they got it right. Before long, they tread a well-worn path around the house.

Earl was making great strides in timing and tone, but he continued to pick with two fingers. He still dreamed of adding a third. To someone with Earl's superb musical ear, the sound of the two-finger technique was unsatisfying. The music sounded too jerky, with abrupt starts and stops. Three fingers would make the music flow.

Earl's Eureka Moment

At age ten, Earl and Horace got into a fight. Lula Scruggs sent them to separate rooms. Earl was sulking in the living room picking "Reuben" on the banjo to make himself feel better. Distracted, his mind still bothered by the argument, he wasn't focusing on what his fingers were doing. Suddenly, he realized he was playing with three fingers.

He jumped up and ran around the house crying, "I've got it! I've got it! I can play with three fingers!"

Adding the middle finger to the thumb and index finger made the melody sound much smoother. Years later, he recalled in his book:

> *I found that the melody line had...been smoothed out, had become less jerky and flowed easily from one note to the next in a continuous regular pattern, rather than jumping and jerking along...The thing that most impressed me...was here was a way...of achieving the graceful fiddle style on the banjo. The notes would flow, just like they did on a fiddle. I started working on it in earnest.*

The rest of the week, he practiced "Reuben" with three fingers to get the flowing pattern he wanted. He played it over and over, perfecting his technique.

At first, Earl's three-finger playing did not sound as good to him as the other three-finger banjoists in the area. But he was pleased he could play songs he'd never been able to before. The three-finger style worked well with both fast and slow songs, which delighted Earl.

Earl's Three-Finger Playing Blossoms

In 1935, when Earl was eleven, he had another chance to play on the radio. Early one morning, he, Horace and Earl's friend T.W. Bryant piled into T.W.'s father's Model T Ford. Mr. Bryant drove the trio to Spartanburg,

South Carolina, to play on WSPA's 7:00 a.m. talent show. Eleven-year-old Earl's three-finger picking woke up folks across the region.

In 1937, at thirteen, Earl bought his first banjo. He rustled up $10.95 to order one from a mail-order catalogue. When the postman brought the package to the Scruggs farm, Earl lost no time opening it. Years later, he still remembered how it smelled when he first unwrapped it.

Earl played his new banjo every chance he could. His mother was a fan but a critic, too. In a 2000 NPR interview, he recalled her telling him, "Earl, if you're going to play something, play something that has a tune to it."

His mother's advice hit him "like a sledgehammer." From then on, he was careful not to overplay songs and to play the melody line clear and strong.

A MUSICIAN, NOT A COMEDIAN

Beginning around 1937, when he was still thirteen, Earl had a regular gig playing dances at Ollie Moore's Fish Camp. Ollie Moore, a worker from Lily Mills in Shelby, owned the building along the banks of the Broad River and rented it out for fish fries and private parties. Earl earned three dollars playing solo for an evening's square dance.

Millworkers and farmers and their wives, up to eighty people, danced to the sounds of teenage Earl Scruggs's mail-order banjo. Playing for hours on end built stamina and was great practice. Dancers needed the music to keep perfect time. With no band to fall back on, Earl had to play the bass line and keep time himself. There was no electricity, so there were no microphones or amps. To be heard, Earl had to learn to pick with force.

In 1939, fifteen-year-old Earl joined a local band called the Carolina Wildcats. He played with it for almost a year. On Saturday mornings, the band played on a radio station in nearby Gastonia. Years later, in his book, Earl remembered his early taste of fame: "It was fun to arrive at the station and read the fan mail (which usually consisted of letters from our relatives)."

On Saturday nights, Earl often played at house parties with Dennis Butler, a World War I veteran who was a fine old-time fiddler. Deep into the night, they played in the doorway of the host's two front rooms, with the furniture removed for dancing.

Playing at these house parties—mostly for fun and practice—gave Earl the chance to improve his backup banjo and lead banjo breaks. He was fascinated by how the banjo and fiddle played off each other. Folks in and

Thirteen-year-old Earl playing for a dance. *Drawing by Tracy Bigelow Grisman, 2015.*

around Flint Hill took increasing notice of him. With Earl on banjo, they knew the dancing would be lively and the music great.

At fifteen, Earl still dreamed of becoming a famous banjoist, but he was uncertain. Banjo players were expected to be comedians. They hammed it up on stage, a holdover from the old minstrel shows. Some string bands still included blackface acts. But as Earl explained years later to author Nicholas Dawidoff, he was too shy to clown it up on stage: "I didn't know if I'd make it or not. I wasn't comedy-oriented. Just didn't know whether I'd be accepted working for somebody when the only talent I had was playing the banjo."

EARL'S FAMILY GETS THEIR FIRST RADIO

Around this same time, 1939, Earl's family got a Sears Roebuck radio. It was the golden age of radio, and Earl, his mother and his siblings still living at home tuned into their favorite programs. One of them was the *Grand Ole Opry* on WSM out of Nashville. At that time, both Charlotte and Atlanta were bigger country music centers than Nashville. Nearby Charlotte was home to WBT, North Carolina's first commercial radio station and one of the Southeast's biggest stations.

The Scruggses, like many farming and millworker families, were fans of a show on WBT called *Crazy Barn Dance*. Each week, the show's touring talent contest went to a different local auditorium and featured aspiring local acts. Fans loved that the show was broadcast live.

In the 1930s, hundreds of string band groups performed live on Charlotte's WBT. Many of these groups also cut records in Charlotte for RCA-Victor and Decca. Earl Scruggs was growing up less than fifty miles from a country music boomtown.

And Earl was making the most of it. He soaked in the local groups that got their start on WBT, like J.E. Mainer's Mountaineers. Wade Mainer on banjo was an inspiring role model for Earl. Earl also loved others playing live on the station, including Bill and Charlie Monroe and the Carter Family.

WIS out of Columbia, South Carolina, featured another of Earl's favorites: banjoist Fisher Hendley of Fisher Hendley and the Aristocratic Pigs. A meatpacking company sponsored the group. Earl loved it when Fisher and one of his Pigs played banjo and fiddle tunes.

Earl also listened to pop music on the radio, including the jazzy big band sounds. Bluegrass banjoist and historian Jim Mills thinks jazz had a big impact on Earl. Mills remembers his own upbringing in Raleigh, North Carolina, when old-timers told him that that if he wanted to play three-finger banjo, he should learn "In the Mood" by Glenn Miller first.

DeWitt "Snuffy" Jenkins and His Bubbling Banjo

One of Earl's favorite musicians to listen to on the radio—and one who would serve as a powerful role model—was banjoist and comedian from nearby Harris, North Carolina, DeWitt "Snuffy" Jenkins (1908–1990). Earl had first met him at Earl's first fiddlers' convention when Earl was six and Snuffy was twenty-two.

Earl was impressed with Snuffy's fluid, three-finger style. Snuffy used a three-finger "roll," a repeating sequence picked with the thumb, index and middle finger to create a bubbling, syncopated sound. Snuffy's roll flowed better than anyone else's. Snuffy was rooted in old-time music but was giving it a new, peppy drive.

In 1927, when he was nineteen, Snuffy met Smith Hammett and heard him play. According to banjoist and music historian Bob Carlin, Snuffy joined Hammett in a band. Snuffy was delighted by Hammett's three-finger banjo rolls and soaked in his three-finger technique. In a letter Smith Hammett's grandson Larry Hammett shared with Bob Carlin, Snuffy wrote, "As far as I'm concerned, Smith Hammett was the first man to come out with the three-finger style playing…he was the first one that I heard do it. There's a lot of people give me credit, but that is not true."

But Snuffy was the first in the region to broadcast the three-finger style over the airwaves. In 1934, he led the Jenkins String Band on WBT's *Crazy Barn Dance*. To be heard better over the radio, he used metal finger picks, very rare at the time. The publicity for his band boasted it was "playing the old-time mountain tunes like very few can, and in that 'peppy' style that is peculiarly their own."

Banjoist Tony Trischka believes Snuffy's three-finger technique was the style toward which Charlie Poole was heading had he lived. According to Trischka, "Snuffy became the man to take the three-finger style to the doorstep of bluegrass."

In 1936, Snuffy joined J.E. Mainer's Mountaineers on WIS in Columbia, South Carolina, replacing Wade Mainer on banjo. The show had inspired many up-and-coming musicians with its fast-paced, forward-driving sound. In 1937, J.E. Mainer's Mountaineers cut a record for RCA in a makeshift recording studio on the top floor of the Hotel Charlotte.

Snuffy was an amazingly powerful model for young musicians. By 1939, fifteen-year-old Earl was listening intently to him on the radio and attending his live shows. Also at the shows was another young, crackerjack three-finger banjoist from North Carolina: Don Reno (1927–1984). Earl and Don studied Snuffy so they could emulate his technique.

But as Snuffy recalled in an interview with Tony Trischka, "I don't claim to have taught Earl or Don, either one, anything."

Both Earl and Don probably thought otherwise, but Snuffy insisted:

> *It's gotta be born in you, I think. You got it or you don't have it. But I was always willing to* [show] *anyone anything. I could do it and let them pick it up in a short time…They'd come around to where we was playing in a show date and, naturally, I'd show them whatever I could if they wanted me to.*

THE MORRIS BROTHERS OPEN THE DOOR

One evening in 1939, Earl hopped into the passenger seat of a Model A Ford coupe and headed to Chesnee, South Carolina. He was on his way to a concert in a high school auditorium featuring a hot band he listened to on the radio: the Morris Brothers.

Earl drove down at the urging of Grady Wilkie. Wilkie was a friend of Earl's mother, and his uncle Dewey McDaniel had been a fellow millworker and bandmate of Smith Hammett.

Grady Wilkie viewed Earl as one of the best three-finger banjo pickers around. Even though Earl was only fifteen, Wilkie thought he had a shot with the pros. He knew that Don Reno, who was even younger than Earl, had recently played with the Morris Brothers. Wilkie had never met the brothers, but he was determined to introduce them to Earl.

The Morris Brothers were one of the best-liked groups in the Carolinas. Wiley Morris (1919–1990) and Claude "Zeke" Morris (1916–1999) hailed from a musical farm family from Old Fort, North Carolina, near Asheville. In the mid-1930s, they headed to the Charlotte area to make it as musicians. Their older brother George had joined them. They made a small income through recordings, radio shows and, most of all, live appearances.

The Morris Brothers embodied the key elements of what would soon be called "bluegrass." By 1938, the brothers had put together what would become known as the basic bluegrass band: fiddle, guitar, mandolin and banjo played in the three-finger style. In 1938, they had a huge hit with their arrangement of "Let Me Be Your Salty Dog."

Traveling around the Carolinas at the same time as the Morris Brothers were two brothers from Kentucky, Bill and Charlie Monroe. The Monroe and Morris brothers met each other through radio work. They became friends. Though the Morris Brothers helped pave the way, it was Bill Monroe (1911–1996) who would become known as the "Father of Bluegrass."

Probably more excited than anyone to hear the Morris Brothers play at the packed auditorium that night was Grady Wilkie. Grady admired Zeke's rapid-fire mandolin playing and the expert guitar work of Wiley and George. Grady was eager to try to introduce himself and his young friend. He didn't know what to expect, but the risk of refusal was worth it.

Before the show, Grady went with Earl to the back stage door. Earl stood back a bit as Grady built up his nerve to knock. Friendly guys with an easy-going outlook, Wiley and Zeke opened the door.

Standing in front of them was a stranger in a blue shirt and overalls. Grady Wilkie greeted the brothers and told them the young fellow with him played a great banjo. Earl, also in overalls, slowly walked forward. In a 1980 interview with Wayne Erbsen, Zeke Morris recalled:

> [Earl] *came in and tuned his banjo to my guitar, and he could play as good that night as he can now, if not better. He was just shaky and nervous...I'd have thought he'd have missed everything on the banjo, but he didn't miss a string. So we hired him that night and paid him twenty dollars a week.*

Earl loved having the brothers as mentors, and his playing became faster and more fluid every day. For a number of months in 1939, Earl played with the Morris Brothers on their show on Spartanburg's WSPA, from 6:00 to 7:00 a.m. Pre-dawn, he'd arrive at the station with a pasteboard box filled with his mother's homemade biscuits, jams and jellies.

PREWAR PICKING

In 1941, when Earl was seventeen, he was playing with the local trio the Orange Blossom Hillbillies and earning money from local gigs. He set his eyes on a better banjo. One day, Earl emerged from a pawnshop, beaming and holding his new banjo—a Gibson RB11 he'd bought for around fifty dollars. Instead of being an open back like the mail-order banjos he'd been playing, his new Gibson was a closed-back resonator style, which produced more volume and a richer, deeper tone.

Earl's new banjo sounded great when he played with the Orange Blossom Hillbillies on Spartanburg's WSPA on Saturdays at 8:00 a.m. The booming banjo wowed crowds when the group played at special local events, such as the opening celebration for the Clyde Bridges Grocery and Amoco Station.

In 1942, at age eighteen, Earl Scruggs graduated from Boiling Springs High School just as America entered World War II. Many young men Earl's age proudly signed up to serve. But his father was dead and his older brothers and sisters were no longer living at home. Since Earl had to take care of his widowed mother and a younger half sister, he got a draft deferment.

WARTIME AT LILY MILLS

The Scruggs farm was failing. When Lula Scruggs called her friend Grady Wilkie, she told him the family was close to starving.

She asked Grady to help Earl get a job at Lily Mills, the thread mill in Shelby where he worked. Grady was glad to help. He not only got Earl a job at Lily, but he also invited him to board with him and his family so Earl could be closer to the mill.

At Lily, Earl earned forty cents an hour. To earn more money, for the next three years he often worked seventy-two-hour weeks. The work was loud, boring and tiring. But Earl didn't complain. It was a shorter day than working on the farm.

Earl felt good about supporting his mother and half sister, as well as his country. As he later explained to Nicholas Dawidoff:

> One reason I didn't leave the mill—it was only paying forty cents an hour—was I didn't want to leave home. The other was I didn't feel right leaving a job making thread for the Army during the war. They needed more help. A lot of guys were away fighting.

But millwork was wearing him down. At one point, a doctor ordered him to take a week off. He spent some of his break in Asheville, playing on an early morning radio show with Carl Story, a fine fiddler from Lenoir.

At work, banjo tunes constantly filled his head. Years later, in an interview with Joe Depriest of the *Charlotte Observer*, Earl recalled, "Most of the time, whether I was doffing or spinning, I was thinking about music. I couldn't get it off my mind."

During his three years at Lily, he couldn't tour much, but he played both at home and at work. There was a lot of music-making at the mill, typically after work and during breaks. Earl enjoyed playing at work with Grady Wilkie. Years later, Earl told the *Tennessean*:

> Me and Grady Wilkie would sit in the backseat of my '36 Chevy and play music. He'd play guitar and I'd play banjo until they'd motion us to come back into the mill. That's when I finally realized that what I was doing was of interest to other people. They'd stand around and watch us pick. One of them hadn't heard nothing like that before, and he took his hat off, threw it on the ground and said, "Hot damn!"

Some co-workers told Earl that his banjo could be a ticket out of the mill. But Earl wasn't sure. Earl loved Flint Hill and adored his mother and siblings. Millwork was a grind, but it was steady work. It unnerved him to think of leaving home for the music world.

"LOST JOHN" MILLER AND THE ALLIED KENTUCKIANS

When the war ended in 1945, production at the mill decreased, and Earl no longer felt a patriotic duty to work there. With his mother's encouragement, Earl decided to quit his job at Lily Mills.

Soon, he traveled with a local band to Knoxville, Tennessee, to audition for a show on WNOX. The station didn't hire the group, but a bandleader who played on the station, "Lost John" Miller, heard Earl and asked him to join him. Within a couple of weeks, Earl was traveling with "Lost John" Miller and the Allied Kentuckians. He was earning fifty dollars a week, almost double what he'd been earning working at the mill.

Every Saturday morning, the band would do a radio show on Nashville's WSM. While in Nashville, Earl saw a friend from North Carolina, fiddler Jim Shumate. One Saturday morning, Earl met Shumate in the coffee shop of the Tulane Hotel. Shumate was a huge fan of Earl's banjo picking and urged him to try out for his band, Bill Monroe and His Blue Grass Boys. The Blue Grass Boys were in Nashville for their Saturday evening gig on the *Grand Ole Opry*.

Earl knew the Blue Grass Boys were one of the best string bands out there. But he hesitated to leave his first full-time music job, especially so soon. Shortly after, on December 1, 1945, Miller told his bandmates that he was quitting touring full time. Earl quickly called Shumate and told him he needed a job.

EARL JOINS BILL MONROE AND HIS BLUE GRASS BOYS

Within a matter of days, Jim Shumate arranged for Earl to go to Bill Monroe's hotel room to try out for the Blue Grass Boys. Earl auditioned with

Earl Scruggs (right) with Lester Flatt, at WDVA, Danville, Virginia, 1947. *Photo courtesy of the North Carolina Museum of History/Jim Shumate.*

two songs: the old-time classic "Sally Goodin'" and the less-played "Dear Old Dixie."

Also in the room that day was a former millworker from Tennessee, Lester Flatt (1914–1979). He was the group's guitarist, lead singer and master of ceremonies. Neither of the group's two prior banjo players had impressed him. They'd played too slowly in the clawhammer and two-finger style and had doubled as cornpone comedians. Lester Flatt didn't even think the Blue Grass Boys needed a banjo player.

When Lester heard Earl play with such skill and speed, he changed his mind. Earl was a different animal. In an interview years later with Neil Rosenberg, Lester recalled being "just dumb-founded. I had never heard anybody pick a banjo like he did. He could go all over the neck and do things you couldn't hardly believe." Flatt advised Monroe to hire Scruggs "whatever it costs."

Bill Monroe could see for himself that Earl's fine three-finger picking would fit in well with his band. He offered Earl the job at sixty dollars a week.

Earl was excited to be offered a job with one of the most popular acts on the Grand Ole Opry. But, as Earl explained to Nicholas Dawidoff, he had mixed feelings:

> *By nature, I was a homeboy. I missed Carolina, missed my mother. I was tired of living in hotels. But at the time, I didn't have a job back in the mill at Shelby, so I thought I'd try it for a few months and see. I was at an age when I enjoyed trying new things.*

His first show as a member of the Blue Grass Boys was on December 8, 1945, on the *Grand Ole Opry*.

It was a double thrill for Earl because he was performing in front of a large live audience at the Ryman Auditorium in Nashville, and the show was being carried live over much of the nation. Since 1939, the Opry audience had loved the Blue Grass Boys. What was new that night was the crackerjack three-finger banjoist from North Carolina, twenty-one-year-old Earl Scruggs.

As soon as Bill Monroe and his group started playing with Earl, the crowd went wild. Earl was an instant sensation. The audience gasped when they heard him play solos at breakneck speed. The outpouring of syncopated notes. The banjo playing the melody line. A banjoist who was a virtuoso musician and not a comedian.

People in the audience who had heard the band before knew something was different. With Earl, the group was on fire, with Bill Monroe on mandolin, Lester Flatt on guitar, Chubby Wise on fiddle and Cedric Rainwater (Howard Watts) on bass. Earl's awesome three-finger banjo playing had been the missing ingredient.

With Earl Scruggs in the group, Bill Monroe's dream had become a reality. The music had drive and intensity, a modern sound. Individual musicians took solo breaks, like in jazz. Monroe sang in a high tenor, while Flatt, Scruggs and Rainwater sang tight vocal harmonies. What the Blue Grass Boys were playing was not old-time music anymore; it was a new style. Some music scholars have called them the best quintet in country music history. They were the first "bluegrass" group.

The banjo was quickly becoming the star of the show. Before Earl entered the scene, the banjo was mostly used as a rhythm instrument. But Earl played it as a lead instrument, taking solo breaks and doing what the fiddle typically did. Earl played banjo breaks on songs from slow waltzes to mid-tempo duets to speedy breakdowns.

Many people outside of Virginia and the Carolinas were unfamiliar with three-finger banjo pickers. Earl recalled to Neil Rosenberg, "When I started here, no one had heard the three-finger style before. People would gather around me like I was a freak almost."

Earl was not the only three-finger picker out there, but he was the best. Snuffy Jenkins and Don Reno played in a similar style. Don had been out of circulation for a while because he served in World War II. Snuffy, according to Jim Mills, had 90 percent of the basic elements but had two or three notes missing. Earl added the extra notes and syncopation that smoothed out the rolls.

Bluegrass scholar Bill Malone put it this way: "Earl Scruggs...did not invent the style which now bears his name, but he perfected it and carried it to greater technical proficiency than anyone before him."

Before long, the Grand Ole Opry's announcer, Judge George D. Hay, was announcing Earl as "Earl Scruggs and his fancy banjo" and "the boy who makes the banjo talk."

Musically, Earl was a genius. He knew just the right notes to play and when. He played forcefully but not overly so. He was a master of rhythm and created a syncopated, ragtime sound with bluesy and jazzy breaks. His tone was impeccable, and so was his timing.

Earl's arrival to the Grand Ole Opry was in itself great timing. Before Earl joined the Blue Grass Boys, the banjo had been fading from pop and country and western music. The guitar and the mandolin were taking its place. But Earl's riveting technique put the banjo on a new course. Says Bob Carlin, "I would go so far to suggest that the banjo might have disappeared from our culture if it wasn't for Earl Scruggs."

Six days a week at least, the Blue Grass Boys were on the road, playing at radio stations and one-night live shows. They played for fans in coal camps in Kentucky and West Virginia and in towns and cities throughout the Southeast and down into Florida. Eager fans packed into their shows at fairgrounds, school auditoriums and town halls. The group also played at drive-in theaters, where the band stood atop concession stands.

But success came at a cost. The Blue Grass Boys traveled a grueling schedule around the Southeast, sometimes covering up to three thousand miles a week. They rode from gig to gig packed into the front of a nine-passenger customized stretch Chevy limo. Packed in the back were five suitcases and a tent, bleachers and stairs. In a time before interstates, band members took turns driving and sleeping as they traveled bumpy country roads all night long. Monroe tended to run late, so the group often needed to speed down the narrow roads, sometimes getting into accidents.

Scruggs was exhausted. The pressure was wearing him down. As Earl recalled to Nicholas Dawidoff, "With [Monroe's] methods of operation, we were traveling so much I was hardly going to bed."

There was also the matter of song credit. Earl had written a remarkable instrumental, which he really liked and had shared with the group. Monroe had made a tweak or two, slapped his own title on it—"Blue Grass Breakdown"—and released it as his own without duly compensating Earl.

Meanwhile, the new star was almost broke. By the time he took out expenses, Earl had very little to send to his mother and half sister back home. Earl had been with the Blue Grass Boys for twenty-seven months. In early 1948, worn out and with little money saved to show for it, he decided to give his two weeks' notice and return to Shelby to work in the mill.

EARL, LESTER AND THE FOGGY MOUNTAIN BOYS

Shortly after Earl handed in his notice, Lester Flatt did the same. Lester was also exhausted and tired of low pay. But he didn't want to return to millwork. As Earl told Nicholas Dawidoff, "Lester called me and said he had been thinking about it and we wouldn't be happy back in the mill. He suggested we get a job at a radio station in Carolina, closer to home."

Monroe was furious at both of them for leaving. He gave Earl the silent treatment at the time and barely talked to him for twenty years, though he made sure all of Earl's replacements used the same three-finger style. None could match the master.

In April, just weeks after teaming up with Lester, Earl married the smart, slender brunette he'd been dating, Louise Certain. He met Louise in 1946, two weeks after joining the Blue Grass Boys. Louise was a farm girl from outside Nashville working in the city as a bookkeeper. She had been watching him from the third row at the Ryman and loved what she saw and heard. After the show, Earl met Louise, and they soon were a couple. She went on to deftly manage Earl's career for more than half a century.

That spring of 1948, Louise stayed home with Lula Scruggs in Shelby while Earl and Lester launched their group. Another former Blue Grass Boy joined them: fiddler Jim Shumate. In March, the band had its first regular radio show on WDBA in Danville, Virginia. Soon after, it moved to Hickory, North Carolina, to do a show on WHKY.

By the fall, the group had moved to WCYB in the Tennessee border town of Bristol. The superb guitarist Mac Wiseman joined them. They were a huge hit on a mid-day radio show popular with farmers taking a break for lunch—*Farm 'N Fun Time*. Soon, Earl called Louise and asked her to move from Shelby up to Bristol to be with him.

While in Bristol, Earl and Lester named their band the Foggy Mountain Boys. Foggy Mountain didn't exist in real life, but both Lester and Earl loved the Carter Family song "Foggy Mountain Top."

In late 1948, touring through Bristol with Bill Monroe and the Blue Grass Boys was Don Reno. Earl had been eyeing Don's Gibson Granada Mastertone banjo for years, and now Don was interested in trading. Don's gold-plated banjo was in bad shape, with a broken metal section, but Earl loved its tone. The banjo had belonged to two of Earl's heroes, Snuffy Jenkins and Fisher Hendley. Don and Earl made the trade. Earl would go on to play that banjo for the rest of his career.

In 1949, Earl used his new banjo to release a new song. He went back to the instrumental he'd written with the Blue Grass Boys, which Bill Monroe had called "Blue Grass Breakdown." Earl rearranged it slightly and renamed it "Foggy Mountain Breakdown." The song was an instant hit throughout the South. It would go on to become a bluegrass standard and earn two Grammy Awards.

After releasing "Foggy Mountain Breakdown," Flatt and Scruggs and the Foggy Mountain Boys moved from town to town throughout the South, playing to adoring live and radio audiences. The group was always on the go. Traveling with their bass tied to the top of their car, they covered thousands of miles—innovating, sowing seeds and spreading the bluegrass gospel.

LEGACY

Earl performed for the next six decades and inspired millions of young musicians to learn to play "Scruggs-style" banjo.

Earl's outstanding three-finger banjo picking cemented the original bluegrass sound. Though Bill Monroe is called the "Father of Bluegrass," without the shy boy from Flint Hill and "his fancy banjo," bluegrass as we know it would not exist.

Earl breathed new life into the banjo, as the instrument had done for him when he was a four-year-old lonely for his dad.

Earl never forgot the people and community that had given him the banjo. Late in his life, when the Town of Shelby contacted him about creating a center honoring him and his music, he graciously offered to help. The Earl Scruggs Center in Shelby's town square is a tribute to the native son whose banjo artistry transformed millions of lives around the world.

Classic Earl Scruggs Songs

"The Ballad of Jed Clampett" (theme song for *The Beverly Hillbillies*)
"Earl's Breakdown"
"Flint Hill Special"
"Foggy Mountain Breakdown"

Essential Earl Scruggs CDs

Bill Monroe with Lester Flatt and Earl Scruggs: The Original Bluegrass Band
Earl Scruggs Family and Friends
Flatt and Scruggs (1948–1959, 4-CD box set)
Flatt and Scruggs at Carnegie Hall
Foggy Mountain Banjo

Earl Scruggs's North Carolina

Earl Scruggs Center (Shelby)

Earl Scruggs Videos

Earl Scruggs Family and Friends
The Three Pickers

DAVID HOLT

THE HEALING POWER OF MUSIC

At-a-Glance

———◼◆◾———

DATES: b. 1946
INSTRUMENTS: Banjo, guitar, slide guitar, harmonica, vocals (also bones, spoons, mouth bow, jaw harp and paper bag)
MUSIC STYLES: Old-time and acoustic blues
HOME: Asheville, North Carolina
AWARDS: Four Grammy Awards, Uncle Dave Macon Heritage Award, Brown-Hudson Award
LEGACY: As a musician, storyteller, song collector, television host, music historian and educator, David Holt opens the door into North Carolina's old-time and bluegrass music culture.

FROM TEXAS TO CALIFORNIA

David Holt spent the first ten years of his life in central Texas, where his family had roots a century old. In the 1850s, Holt's great-great-grandfather moved there from Alamance County, North Carolina. The Holts did well in Texas. They were an educated clan filled with lawyers and doctors.

One hot summer day when David Holt was about seven, he got an unexpected music lesson. His mother was driving him and his brother home

Photo: Clark Thomas

David Holt, 1979. *Photo by Clark Thomas, folder 10 in the David Holt Collection, Southern Folklife Collection, the Wilson Library, University of North Carolina at Chapel Hill.*

from the grocery store. The boys were angry that she hadn't bought them a jar of Ovaltine that came with a Captain Midnight decoder ring coupon. Their whining made Mrs. Holt livid. She decided it was time to teach them that money didn't grow on trees.

She pulled over to the side of the road and dragged her sons out of the car. There they stood, at the edge of a cotton field stretching as far as the eye could see. Mrs. Holt grabbed them by their ears and marched them over to the foreman of a large group of men picking cotton.

She asked the foreman to let her sons pick cotton so they could learn the value of work. The foreman agreed and gave each boy a ten-foot-long cotton sack. When their fingers bled and they started to cry under the scorching August sun, the foreman came up behind them and began singing, "There's a long white road in heaven I know, I don't want it to leave me behind." About one hundred African American field hands joined in. The Holt boys stopped crying, and for the rest of the day, the brothers picked cotton surrounded by the beautiful, melodious voices.

Growing up in Texas, David heard his father and grandfather playing the bones. A century earlier, John Oscar Holt had brought his bones from North Carolina to Texas and had played them throughout the Civil War. From the time he was a baby, David loved their rhythmic clicking sounds. When he was about ten and coordinated enough, he learned from his dad and grandpa how to play them. He held the two bones together and practiced clicking them like castanets.

It was during this period, in 1957, when David's father decided to move his family to California. An inventor and engineer, Mr. Holt seized career opportunities out west. It was the year of *Sputnik*, and California's aerospace industry was growing. At first, David pined away for the ranchlands and cotton fields of Texas and the family members he'd left behind. But soon he fell in love with California. Regular summer visits kept him connected to Texas. Most of the year he spent running on the soft sands and surfing in the roaring waves of the Pacific.

David spent his teenage years in Pacific Palisades, an upscale, seaside suburb north of Los Angeles. At fourteen, he began drum lessons, a typical pursuit for a guy his age. Like many teenagers, he formed a rock band with high school friends. Unlike many teenagers, in just two years, he had a hit 45rpm record, "Ski Storm."

David Holt eventually toured with Doc Watson, and they won a Grammy together. Watson became nothing less than a musical father figure to him. But amazingly, as a teenager in 1964, when David first heard Watson play at the Ash Grove music club in Los Angeles, he wasn't that into it. His heart was in drumming, especially rock and jazz.

In 1965, David graduated from high school as president of the class and enrolled in San Francisco State University as an art major. Living in a dorm, he had left his drum set back home. It was an exciting time to be in San Francisco. In 1965 and 1966, music of all kinds was everywhere. He attended one of the first concerts of the Grateful Dead, a local band. Janis Joplin and Jimi Hendrix lived down the street.

David was having a grand time, but after a couple of years, he took time off from college to figure out what he wanted to do with his life. Elementary school teaching appealed to him. To test the waters, he took a job at a private alternative school in a rural section of Martinez, California.

The first evening there, when he was moving belongings into his classroom, an event happened that changed his life.

ASSAULT UNDER THE STARS

David was standing in the school parking lot looking up at the stars when, out of nowhere and for no reason, attackers appeared and beat him to a pulp. The hoodlums vandalized the school and, before driving away, left David for dead. His girlfriend, who was hiding in the school during the attack, found him and called for help.

As he lay on the pavement near death, David's mind filled with a bright orange light and an intense feeling that "all of life was interconnected."

He also felt something strange given the circumstance: that "love was the building block of the universe."

David had another thought, an unusual one for a guy his age: that life was short and that "the veil of death is very close." He decided that with whatever time he had left, he'd make the most of it.

David's recovery began at the school. A teacher friend introduced him to his collection of 78rpm folk records. Unlike a few years earlier, David was drawn to the music.

The records in his friend's collection that he found the most healing were the old cowboy songs:

> *These cowboy singers were lonely and wounded, like me after the assault. They were finding solace in music, and I was doing that, too. I was attracted to cowboy music, not the rock music of my high school days, because the cowboy music was saying what I was feeling inside.*

He loved the Carl Sandburg song "I Ride an Old Paint" about a cowboy who lost his daughters and wife but was still able to sing "from morning 'til night." This song, and similar ones, became David's lifeline.

ROSES AND REHABILITATION

In 1968, after teaching for the school year, the twenty-two-year-old David moved to the stunning, seaside city of Santa Barbara. The low-key beach setting backed by mountains and hiking trails was therapeutic. To earn money, he took a job as a rose wrangler tending two hundred rose bushes. Each evening, at about five o'clock, David sat in the garden as the roses opened and released their intoxicating scents.

In his free time, David listened to a collection of cowboy recordings he found at the Santa Barbara Public Library, *Authentic Cowboys and Their Western Songs*. Soon, he began to sing them. Having never sung before in his life and with no thought of performance, he saw singing as something to help him feel better.

David's job came with an apartment that shared a thin wall with a psychiatrist's office. He overheard patients talking about how unhappy they were with their lives and careers. It made him think. He made an important decision about his future. Rather than being unhappy when he was older, he wanted to spend his life doing what he loved: singing and playing folk music from America's past.

CARL SPRAGUE: COWBOY MUSIC PIONEER

David took steps to pursue his dream. He drove down the coast to meet with D.K. Wilgus, a folklorist at the University of California at Los Angeles. When David told him about his interest in cowboy songs, Wilgus gave David advice he wasn't expecting: seek out Carl Sprague (1895–1979), the pioneering 1920s cowboy musician from Texas.

David contacted Sprague and arranged to meet him. He headed to Bryan, Texas, and spent a day with Sprague, who was seventy-two. Sprague taught David how to play the basic lick of cowboy guitar and how to play the harmonica cowboy-style. The visit was a turning point for David:

> *Carl Sprague was the first one to record cowboy songs back in 1927, and he was happy to spend the whole day with me. I realized that if you find mentors who are accessible and available, you could learn a lot...It was amazing.*

David Holt (center) with Merle and Doc Watson, Deep Gap, North Carolina, 1985. *Photo by Rob Amberg, courtesy of David Holt.*

RALPH STANLEY'S ADVICE

The following year, in 1969, David enrolled at the University of California at Santa Barbara to study biology and art.

Outside of class, he had discovered another source of vintage, historic recordings at the Santa Barbara Public Library: the *Anthology of American Folk Music* edited by Harry Smith. It consisted of old-time and blues recordings from the 1920s and '30s. David was enthralled by the collection and spent countless hours soaking in the classic tunes.

As great as it was listening to all this old-time music from forty years before, David liked to listen to live music, too. One evening, he went to hear a performance at the university by bluegrass banjoist Ralph Stanley. Stanley was one of the biggest names in bluegrass music. He was born and raised in the mountains of southwest Virginia, and like Sprague, he was the real deal.

David loved the sound of Ralph Stanley's banjo so much that after the show he went backstage. He told Stanley he wanted to learn the old African-derived clawhammer style, with its down-stroking motion that strummed all the strings at once.

Ralph Stanley told him that the best way to learn to play clawhammer banjo was to attend fiddlers' conventions in the southeastern mountains and learn from the old-timers. David tucked the advice into the back of his mind. He didn't realize at the time that it would change his life.

One of David's musician friends in Santa Barbara was Peter Feldman, a bluegrass and old-time musician who was interested in the music's roots. By this time, in 1969, the commercial folk revival had come and gone, and what remained were people like David and Feldman who were digging deeper. When Feldman also suggested visiting fiddlers' conventions in the southern Appalachians, David began making travel plans.

SUMMER IN THE NORTH CAROLINA MOUNTAINS

That summer, when he was twenty-three, David Holt set off for the North Carolina mountains with another young musician friend, Steve Keith. When they arrived, David knew they'd come to the right place: "I felt like I had stumbled on a lost continent, the lost continent of traditional music. I was hooked!"

David and Steve spent the summer meeting musicians during the week and going to fiddlers' conventions on weekends. They were having the time of their lives. They had loved the music back in California; now they were at its source.

When Steve Keith played clawhammer banjo, local musicians were intrigued. When he played in front of laundromats and other public spots, he attracted small crowds. By the late 1960s, the more common style of banjo playing was the bluegrass three-finger picking style. The only people playing clawhammer in the mountains were the old guys, and they weren't playing it much in public.

Watching Steve Keith, David Holt became more intent than ever to master clawhammer banjo. It would be his entrée into the world of the old mountain musicians. Back in California at the end of the summer, he focused on clawhammer technique.

Mountain Music Mentors

Three years later, in the summer of 1972, David returned to the North Carolina mountains, this time with his future wife, fellow University of California at Santa Barbara student Ginny Callaway. Now a fine clawhammer banjoist, David found that he and Ginny were welcomed into the homes of older musicians. From these seasoned players, David learned old tunes and mountain ways.

The eighty- and ninety-year-old North Carolina mountain musicians who became his mentors and friends were born in the late 1800s. They'd grown up before radios and records. David admired their self-sufficiency, wisdom and "centeredness." To him, it seemed that they "grew up before self-doubt was invented." They knew how to grow a garden, fix a roof and tend to the sick.

Many of these smart mountain old-timers didn't have schooling beyond the third grade. That intrigued him. What happened to intelligence when people stopped their schooling? He decided it went to unusual places. For these old mountain musicians, it had been channeled into mind-boggling musical skill. They had the ability, played with passion and were master musicians. David knew that to even get close to their level would demand enormous time and focus.

At summer's end, David and Ginny returned to California. By June 1973, David was twenty-seven and finishing college with undergraduate degrees in biology and art and a graduate certificate in elementary school teaching. He also had a job offer in Santa Barbara at the highest-paid elementary school in the United States. But he turned it down to move back to North Carolina for good.

In the 1850s, his great-great-grandfather had left North Carolina for Texas. Now, David was moving back. The cycle would be complete.

That summer, soon after graduation, he and Ginny headed to the southern mountains.

North Carolina Music Transplant

By this time, America had been engulfed in the Vietnam War for almost a decade. A growing number of young people were distrustful of politicians. The dominant culture was saying: believe those in control, buy commercial products and adopt mainstream values. But many young people were looking for a less militaristic, less commercial path. They were embracing a down-to-earth lifestyle.

Some of these young people, including David, were drawn more to music than to politics. For these young folks, North Carolina offered what they were searching for: realness, roots and great music.

Most of the transplants were middle-class college graduates. Many were from cities and suburbs in the Northeast, and many looked like hippies. In addition to the music, they were drawn to other aspects of Appalachian culture, such as how to keep a beehive, make moonshine and cure ailments with natural remedies.

In Surry County, David met transplants from around the country who gathered around the old-time fiddler and banjo player Tommy Jarrell. As seen in chapter two, Jarrell was in his early seventies and was very welcoming to his young visitors. Day and night, David and other transplants played music, danced and talked in Jarrell's small house. David soaked in clawhammer techniques from Jarrell and Fred Cockerham, another fine local banjoist and fiddler.

Jarrell, Cockerham and other older musicians from the area loved David and the other young visitors, who in turn loved and respected them. It was a great match.

Many of the area's more educated, wealthier residents looked down on the local old-time musicians who had less money and schooling. But to the transplants, these older musicians were heroes.

David and the other transplants hadn't liked the smooth, commercial folk music of Peter, Paul and Mary; the Kingston Trio; and other urban folk groups of the 1950s and early '60s. They preferred the grittier, southern field recordings made by folklorists such as Ralph Rinzler and Mike Seeger. Some transplants, like David, had heard musicians such as Ralph Stanley and Doc Watson in music clubs and on college campuses. Now, in Surry County, the transplants were learning the gritty, driving music they loved from some of the world's best players.

ASHEVILLE HOME

Toward the end of 1973, after spending months in Surry County, David and Ginny moved to Asheville. In those days, Asheville was not the hip, artsy and glamorous city it is today. Much of the downtown was boarded up. What grabbed David was the city's friendly people and its old-time and bluegrass culture. Of special interest was the Mountain Dance and Music Festival, *the* folk festival at the time. It was the brainchild of a well-known lawyer and folklorist, Bascom Lamar Lunsford, whom David had met.

Settled in Asheville, David earned money as a sign painter. At night, he practiced his music. He soon began performing locally. With his beaming smile and his ease at telling stories and singing songs to children, David was a hit in schools.

Before long, the local newspaper ran a feature article on him. As a young person who had moved from California and was playing old-time music, David was a novelty. Many people around town first heard of David Holt through the article.

Encouraged by the good press, David threw himself into the area's old-time music scene. Two years later, in 1975, at age twenty-nine, he founded the Appalachian Music Program at Warren Wilson College in nearby Swannanoa. It was the first program of its kind and continues to this day. Graduates of the program, such as Laura Boosinger, have become stars of North Carolina's old-time music scene. David started Warren Wilson's Mountain Music Archive. Today, it is available online in the "Music" section of the Digital Library of Appalachia.

BLUE RIDGE RENAISSANCE MAN

In 1980, five years after starting the program at Warren Wilson College, David began hosting his *Folkways* series on UNC-TV. David was a natural for TV—learned, friendly and verbal. He interviewed the mountain musicians he loved and played favorite songs with them. The mountain folk felt relaxed and happy around him, and David made their music and culture accessible to viewers. David's genial nature worked well for his other main activity that year: his first international musical tour for the U.S. Department of State.

In 1981, at age thirty-five, David left Warren Wilson College to begin a full-time performing career. He released his first record. In 1982, he made his first appearance on the *Grand Ole Opry*. From 1984 to 1989, he hosted the *Fire on the Mountain* TV series. From 1985 to 1994, he made over twenty-five guest appearances on *Hee Haw*. He went on to host other TV series: *Celebration Express* and *American Music Shop*.

David Holt, Deep Gap, North Carolina, 2003. *Photo by Tim Barnwell, courtesy of David Holt.*

But just as everything was going well professionally for Holt, the ground fell out from under him. In 1989, his ten-year-old daughter, Sara Jane, died in a car accident. The loss left him so shattered that he didn't want to live. Learning how to play the blues on steel guitar became his lifeline. Merle Watson had once given him a blues guitar lesson, and David built on that foundation. According to David, "Cowboy songs gave me a way to live. Blues gave me a reason to live."

Since 1989, David has performed acoustic blues as well as old-time music for adoring audiences around North Carolina and the world. He plays standards in each genre, as well as his own songs. His solo shows are absorbing and unique. He performs on a wide variety of instruments, educates the audience on the instruments and songs and shares stories and photos of the musicians he has befriended over the years.

David has also created and performed in many groups. From 1998 to 2012, he toured with Doc Watson, whom he considered his "musical father." Their work together resulted in the Grammy Award–winning album *Legacy*. The album tells the stories of Doc Watson's life through spoken word and song.

David has also performed with his son Zeb and Laura Boosinger (David Holt and the Lightning Bolts), Josh Goforth (David Holt and Josh Goforth) and Bryan Sutton and T. Michael Coleman (Sutton, Holt and Coleman).

David's *Stellaluna* CD earned him two Grammy Awards for storytelling.

For four decades, David has made on-site recordings of musicians singing songs and telling tales. They are now part of the permanent collections of the University of North Carolina at Chapel Hill and the Library of Congress.

In 2015, David launched a new series on UNC-TV called *David Holt's State of Music*. It showcases David performing with some of North Carolina's finest young bluegrass and old-time talent. The series is a tribute to his adopted home state and its new music masters.

MUSIC AS MEDITATION AND THERAPY

Over the years, David has put in countless hours of practice. According to him, practice has played a central role in his life:

> *To learn music and have it become part of you, you have to play it over and over to build your muscle memory…You need to find a way to love the nuances of the music, to inhabit the notes, so it becomes part of you. When I practice music, I am in a state of being very aware of what I am doing. I sort of float off in this state.*

For David, practicing music is not only a form of meditation; it's also a form of therapy: "Music can go down to the sad, deep places in you and then bring you back up. It sinks way down inside and helps you find some hope at the end."

LEGACY

David Holt had the smarts, education and means to become anything he wanted. In the wake of a brutal attack, he decided to commit his life to what soothed, healed and intrigued him. It was a decision that has served him and others well. Through his performances, recordings and TV shows,

David has emerged a musical Renaissance man who uplifts, inspires and enlightens. When asked what he wants his legacy to be, he replied:

> *I want to be remembered as a good musician and a good friend who opened the door to many other people to appreciate North Carolina's mountain music culture. It's been tremendously valuable to me, and I hope it is tremendously valuable to somebody else after I am gone. If I can have had a hand in future generations discovering it, I will feel great. I will feel satisfied.*

No one has done more to preserve and promote North Carolina's old-time and bluegrass music culture than David Holt. He has been making the most of the time he's had, and he's still going strong.

North Carolina is lucky to have him. And according to David, "I'm so lucky to have North Carolina."

David Holt's Favorite Songs

Banjo: "Bound to Ride"
Guitar: "Ready for the Times to Get Better"
Steel Guitar: "Steel Guitar Blues"

Essential David Holt CDs

David Holt and the Lightning Bolts
Let It Slide
Ready for the Times (by Sutton, Holt and Coleman)

David Holt's Asheville

Mountain Dance and Folk Festival: This event began in 1928 and is the sister event to Shindig on the Green.

Shindig on the Green: This event in downtown Asheville, which began in 1967, features a stage show and informal jam sessions on Saturday evenings in the summer. David Holt has been taking part over the years and plays there whenever he can.

David Holt, Asheville, North Carolina, 2005. *Photo by Tim Barnwell, courtesy of David Holt.*

Swannanoa Gathering: These weeklong summer workshops at Warren Wilson College near Asheville teach banjo, fiddle, guitar and more to students of all ages.

David Holt's Website

DavidHolt.com

RHIANNON GIDDENS

CAROLINA CHOCOLATE DROP

At-a-Glance

———◆◆◆———

DATES: *b. 1977*

INSTRUMENTS: *Vocals, banjo, fiddle, kazoo*

MUSIC STYLES: *Old-time (with a focus on African American string band music from the 1920s and '30s) country blues, early jazz, jug band, spirituals*

HOME: *Greensboro, North Carolina*

AWARDS: *Grammy Award*

LEGACY: *Rhiannon is a rising star who keeps African American old-time music alive. A founding member of the Carolina Chocolate Drops, she's a multitalented performer with an operatically trained voice. She resurrects great forgotten songs from America's past and interprets them in new and exciting ways.*

CITY GIRL, COUNTRY GIRL

Rhiannon Giddens was born in Greensboro into a family with a passion for music. Rhiannon and her older sister, Lalenja, loved singing with their parents, especially folk songs. The family of four didn't have a lot of money, but they had high-quality phonograph speakers. Music from gospel to classical guitar flowed through their home.

Rhiannon Giddens (with Dom Flemons in the background), American Tobacco campus, Durham, North Carolina, 2009. *Photo by Bernard Thomas, courtesy of the* Herald-Sun.

Both parents grew up in the country east of Greensboro and moved to the city for college. At the University of North Carolina at Greensboro, they joined the campus hippie scene. They loved the 1950s and '60s folk revival singers like Joan Baez, Judy Collins and Peter, Paul and Mary.

The civil rights movement was more important to Rhiannon's parents than to many other young people. Rhiannon's mother was African American, and her father was white.

By and large, Rhiannon thrived in a nurturing family setting. Being a biracial family had its strains. Despite the tensions, Rhiannon's extended families on both sides were loving. Her parents were devoted to her and Lalenja.

From age one to second grade, while her mother went back to college to complete her degree, Rhiannon lived with her maternal grandparents outside Greensboro in the country. When she was eight, she moved back to town. From then on, she spent weekends in Julian with her father's parents and in Sedalia with her mother's.

Rhiannon's maternal grandparents farmed an acre of land. She loved the many hours she spent in their yard, surrounded by the green lawn, scuppernong grapes and the smell of fresh country air. Rhiannon ran around the big oak tree with her sister and cousins. After hours of outdoor fun, the children would scurry into the kitchen and soak in the aromas of food their grandmother was making from scratch. Years later, memories of these happy times would show up in the lyrics Rhiannon wrote for her popular song "Country Girl."

BLESSED WITH MULTIPLE GIFTS

Rhiannon was no ordinary child. Good at right and left brain pursuits, she was top of her class in arts and academics. She was an avid reader with a special interest in historical novels. Jane Austen was one of her favorite authors.

In her junior and senior years of high school, she went to the North Carolina School of Science and Math in Durham. Only the most gifted students in the state were accepted into this rigorous, free, science and math boarding school. Though she had talent in graphic arts, Rhiannon's plan was to pursue quantum physics.

Then she discovered her love for singing. She started a choral group at school, and the summer after her junior year, she went to a choral camp at the selective Governor's School of North Carolina. Encouraged by her teachers there, she decided to apply to a college in Oberlin, Ohio. It was one of the most prestigious music schools in the country: the Oberlin Conservatory of Music.

OPERA TRAINING AT OBERLIN

Rhiannon arrived at Oberlin in 1995, mingling with classmates who had been immersed in classical music since birth. She studied opera performance, soaking it all up like a kid in a candy store. A self-described "quintessential nerd," she excelled. Rhiannon took a range of courses, including aural skills and music theory. She sampled extracurriculars, such as contra dance, and spun around with classmates to the lively sounds of the music. She had lead roles in a number of productions and sang off campus with professional companies, including the Cleveland Opera.

Rhiannon's voice teacher was from New York. Growing up in the South, Rhiannon was used to the half-hour goodbye. Rhiannon thought her teacher hated her because of the hasty way she would say goodbye to Rhiannon after class. It took Rhiannon a while to realize that it was typical for a New Yorker to say goodbye quickly and that her teacher liked her and saw her as a talented singer headed for a great opera career.

In 2000, she left Oberlin with a bachelor of music, not at all sure she wanted to enter the intense opera world. She knew it would be constantly competitive and would wear her down. Feeling burned out, she decided to take a break.

BACK HOME IN NORTH CAROLINA

Rhiannon was happy to return to North Carolina. She enjoyed her time at Oberlin and learned a lot there, but it wasn't home. She'd missed the South.

She was glad to be back in a place where people waved even if they didn't know you. She was happy to reconnect with family and old friends. She savored eating biscuits, fried chicken and sweet potato pie again. She had missed them when she was living up North.

Returning home to Greensboro, Rhiannon went to work to pay the bills. A crackerjack typist with computer and graphic design skills, she had no trouble getting temp jobs in companies around town. Soon she landed a permanent job, working her way up to assistant to the CEO.

THE WORLD OF CONTRA DANCING

In the evenings after work, Rhiannon went contra dancing. She hadn't been able to get as involved with it at Oberlin, with her busy class schedule and opera rehearsals. She was learning that there was a statewide contra dance scene in North Carolina and was eager to do more dancing now that she had the time.

When Rhiannon saw the flyer for contra dancing at Oberlin, she thought it was genteel English country dancing out of a Jane Austen novel. What she found was an American offshoot similar to square dancing but with more whirling around, lining up in rows and changing dance partners.

The first contra dance Rhiannon attended in North Carolina was run by the Fiddle and Bow Country Dancers in Winston-Salem. She loved it and, before long, became a self-proclaimed "dance gypsy," attending contra dances at least three times a week in places like Durham, Charlotte and Asheville. She'd see other dance gypsies at each dance. She enjoyed the communal dance aspect—linking arms and dancing with a variety of partners. She also liked the music—Celtic troupes and old-time bands.

Rhiannon needed the boost contra dancing gave her. Though she was doing well at work, she was depressed. She felt overwhelmed, uncertain about her musical direction and almost every other aspect of her life.

With her operatic aspirations on hold, the less formal, less cutthroat world of contra dancing was just what she needed to lift her spirits. Rhiannon liked the free-spirited counter-culture crowd. Everyone fit in, especially "nerds." It was a safe place with no drinking. There was a mix of generations. Contra dancing had no soloists, no stars. She wasn't expected to stand out. All she had to do was dance in time with the other dancers in the room. She got involved with contra dance weekend retreats. Before long, she began calling dances, shouting out: "Swing to your right! Swing to your left!"

DRAWN TO OLD-TIME

At the contra dances, Rhiannon heard some of North Carolina's best old-time string bands. She was familiar with bluegrass and country through her father's family, but old-time music was new to her. She found herself drawn to the sounds of old-time fiddle and banjo.

Rhiannon was attracted to old-time music for several reasons. It was functional—dance music of the common man—and she had discovered it through dancing. It reminded her of the folk music she grew up singing with her parents and sister. A self-described "control freak," she also liked that, unlike opera singers, old-time musicians could decide what, with whom and where they would perform.

On a gut level, she liked the unadorned quality of the music. As a reader of post-apocalyptic fiction, she also liked that old-time was acoustic. People would still be able to make the music even if the stereo speakers stopped working.

She also liked the people. The old-time crowd had a different vibe than the competitive opera scene. Most old-time musicians didn't view music as a full-time profession. Many were college-educated, nerdy and progressive like herself. She was eager to get more involved.

Rhiannon Giddens at MusicFest 'n Sugar Grove, Sugar Grove, North Carolina, 2009. *Photo by Joe Giordano, courtesy Flickr user Appalachian Encounters, https://www.flickr.com/ photos/28744394@N08/3719301322.*

THE LURE OF THE BANJO AND FIDDLE

The fiddle was the first old-time instrument that called her name. She went to David Sheppard's shop in Greensboro, and this wonderful old-time musician and luthier sold Rhiannon her first fiddle. She got formal training from Marta Richardson, a Suzuki violin teacher in town. She studied the fiddlers at the contra dances.

Before long, Rhiannon's fiddle playing was good enough for her to join Gaelwynd, a Celtic band made up of musicians she'd met at a dance. Celtic music was closely related to old-time, as Scotch and Irish music traditions were two of the roots of old-time music. Soon, Rhiannon was also playing the fiddle with old-time musicians she met at dances.

The next step was learning to play the banjo. She borrowed a friend's instrument for three months. Playing it was difficult because it was old and the strings were at the wrong height above the fingerboard. To earn money to buy a new banjo, she worked nights as a singing hostess at the Macaroni Grill. She worked there long enough to earn the money to buy a shiny new Deering Goodtime banjo.

OLD-TIME'S AFRICAN ROOTS

Around this time, a musical friend told her something that rocked her world: old-time music was part African.

She learned that old-time music was a mixture of fiddle music European settlers brought from the British Isles and banjo music that slaves brought from Africa. Until now, she'd thought of old-time music as rural white men picking banjos on their front porches. That was the impression she'd gotten from pop culture and the school history books. She was shocked to learn that the banjo, or a close cousin of it, was an African instrument. When she heard that in 1900 there were as many African American string bands as European-American ones, she was hooked.

Eager to learn as much as she could about the music's African American roots, she attacked the subject head on, as any good nerd would. She read Dr. Cece Conway's four-hundred-page book, *African Banjo Echoes in Appalachia*.

At a contra dance weekend, a friend told her about CDs he'd been listening to featuring historic African American old-time musicians. She started searching out these works and soaking up esoteric albums like *Black Banjo Songsters of North Carolina and Virginia; Etta Baker and Family*; and *Folks, He Sure Do Pull Some Bow!*

She collected books and liner notes, searched online and spent hours in libraries and bookstores. She soaked in all she could about the early black old-time bands and the times in which they lived.

Rhiannon's research challenged myths she'd learned about American history. She was excited and proud to read that the banjo influenced most American musical styles. She was fascinated to learn that the instrument was the first American musical export, with banjo mania spreading around the world, predating rock-and-roll by one hundred years.

The more Rhiannon read about the banjo and black old-time music, the more she learned about contemporary American music. She began to see styles in popular American music as having their roots in the minstrel songs of the 1850s. In the past, when she heard rap, hip-hop and rock, she had asked herself: where did that come from? Now she had some answers.

BLACK OLD-TIME MUSIC AND SELF-DISCOVERY

By learning about history through music, Rhiannon was also learning more about herself. She began to think it was "not so weird" that she, a person of color, enjoyed bluegrass and old-time music. Ancestors on both sides of her racially mixed family had played and loved this kind of music. She was connecting with black old-time music as her music, discovering where she came from.

Many of the nineteenth-century banjo songs she was listening to talked about skin tone. "High tone" meant light-skinned African Americans like herself. Being biracial, skin color had been an issue for Rhiannon from an early age. Her maternal grandmother had often used this same term to describe her.

Rhiannon's attraction to old-time music, passion for history and close connection to her biracial family were pieces of a puzzle now starting to fit together. She was more eager than ever to learn about the black old-time tradition and herself in the process.

Why the Heritage Was Lost

Rhiannon was understanding herself better and understanding American history more fully. Learning about African American old-time music filled in some of the gaps. In school, she'd learned about slavery and the Harlem Renaissance, but what had happened in between? Through her research, she discovered that during this period, there were many talented black old-time bands performing around the country. But why hadn't she learned about them before?

After reading various books and articles, Rhiannon concluded that the white recording industry was largely to blame. In the 1910s and 1920s, when the industry had come into being, it had released African American "ethnic" or "race" records. These "race" records, targeted toward a black audience, contained classic blues songs, not rural old-time tunes.

It was deeply ingrained in the music executives' minds that blacks bought blues while southern rural and small-town whites bought old-time or "hillbilly" music. So when rural black old-time bands came to seek a record deal, the executives asked them, "What blues do you know?" African American musicians had quickly learned that if they wanted to be recorded on the big labels, they needed to play blues. The commercial recording industry, with its expertise in marketing and creating a niche, had codified in the public mindset that old-time music was white and blues was black.

It wasn't only the record industry's doing. For most African Americans of the period, blues was what they wanted to hear. Why was this? Musical tastes

Rhiannon Giddens, Orton Park Festival, Madison, Wisconsin, 2010. *Photo by Ron Wiecki.*

had shifted, as large numbers of African Americans had migrated from the rural South to southern cities and northern industrial areas. Left behind was the demand for country-sounding, southern, old-time songs.

Many blacks had wanted to forget about African American old-time music. Most minstrel performers had been whites wearing blackface. Many of the old songs had featured racist lyrics that lampooned blacks and were painful reminders of the days of slavery and Jim Crow. There had been some black minstrels in blackface who entertained both black and white audiences; it was basically the only way African Americans could make a living in entertainment. Contemporary black audiences had enjoyed the shows, but the next generation of blacks felt embarrassed and ashamed. Even though many of the songs had been terrific musically and stellar lyrically, their racist overtones had made them painful to hear.

It took just a generation for African Americans to forget that its own community had ever played banjo and fiddle music. By the 1930s, African American old-time music had faded from memory.

Rhiannon understood why most older African Americans wanted to look forward, not backward. Rhiannon's grandmother had grown up in the Depression. Her mother had come of age during the civil rights era. They knew the sting of racism.

Rhiannon, on the other hand, had a different view. She had the privilege of an upbringing that did not dwell on questions like, "Can I get a good job?" and "Can I drink from the same water fountain?" Rhiannon, like other young blacks, could look back without pain or shame and appreciate the musical and cultural value of the old black minstrel songs.

Meeting Joe Thompson

One evening in 2001, Rhiannon took a break from poring over books, articles and liner notes about African American old-time history and discovered a live remnant: fiddler Joe Thompson. Rhiannon and her sister Lalenja heard Thompson play near Greensboro. There he was, performing before their very eyes, a "tour de force" musician in his eighties and the last of a long line of African American fiddlers who stretched back to the nineteenth century. Rhiannon had read about him in Cece Conway's book *African Banjo Echoes in Appalachia*. Here he was in the flesh, playing better than any fiddler she'd ever heard.

As we've seen, in the 1970s, a group of scholar-musicians met Thompson and heard him play. They made and issued recordings of Thompson and helped arrange for him to perform publicly. Since the '70s, scholar-musicians continued to visit Thompson and encouraged him to keep fiddling. Joe and his cousin Odell went on to play gigs at the Kennedy Center, Carnegie Hall and other venues around the country and even overseas.

In 2001, soon after Rhiannon heard Thompson play, she visited him at his house in nearby Mebane. Joe and other musicians were having a jam session, and she jumped right in. She was entering a bygone era that Thompson had kept alive, and she loved it. Here was an African American man from the community her maternal grandmother had grown up in who was playing the fiddle, an instrument she'd recently learned to play.

Shortly afterward, Joe Thompson had a stroke, which put him out of commission for a while.

Gaelic Interlude

Rhiannon also kept on singing, playing and researching Celtic music. After all, the music of Scotland and Ireland, brought over by settlers to the

American South, were two important influences in old-time music. Celtic music was, in many ways, old-time minus the African American influences. The music was steeped in history and appealed to many classically trained musicians with its emphasis on string and harp melodies.

In 2004, Rhiannon began to delve deeper into the Celtic world. Two great things happened at the Highland Games at Grandfather Mountain: she won first prize in the Gaelic song competition, and she met Michael Newton, a Gaelic scholar. She soon moved to Richmond, Virginia, to be near him.

Rhiannon's nerdy side was attracted to Michael Newton. He was one of the foremost Scots-Gaelic scholars in North America and fluent in Gaelic. He'd written *We're Indians Sure Enough: The Legacy of Scottish Highlanders in the United States*. Rhiannon was eager to soak up as much as she could about the language and culture that gave context to the music she loved. She'd grown close to one of the world's best Gaelic teachers, and she used her time in Richmond to study Gaelic.

BLACK BANJO GATHERING

As Rhiannon learned more about the Scottish and Irish roots of old-time music, she was also delving deeper into the music's African American roots. A contra dance acquaintance told her about an upcoming gathering at Appalachian State in Boone. Professor Cece Conway was organizing the Black Banjo Gathering. Rhiannon felt excited about the prospect of meeting other African Americans who shared her passion for black old-time music. For the first time, she was thinking about starting an African American old-time band and was eager to meet other musicians who might share her dreams.

Rhiannon went online and learned more about the upcoming conference. She also learned about the online Yahoo discussion group "Black Banjo, Then and Now." Many of the people posting on that group were excited about the upcoming event. Rhiannon contacted Appalachian State, offered it her web design services and was soon designing the conference website.

In April 2005, Rhiannon attended the Black Banjo Gathering, and the mood there was electric. For four days, she met banjo lovers from around the country and world curious about the instrument's African and African American roots. Musicians mixed with folklorists and other academics.

Rhiannon joined them for a lecture here, a talk there. She heard a musician from Gambia playing an ancestor of the banjo called the akonting, followed by an old-timer from Appalachia playing familiar tunes. She soaked up jams in the hallways, excited conversations and new sounds.

JUSTIN ROBINSON AND DOM FLEMONS

For two other young African American musicians, the event was also life changing. One was Justin Robinson, and the other was Dom Flemons. Justin and Dom didn't know each other, and neither of them knew Rhiannon.

Justin Robinson grew up in Gastonia, North Carolina, in a musical family that embraced a wide range of music. Gifted, he played the violin from a young age. At the time of the Gathering, he was an undergraduate at the University of North Carolina at Chapel Hill exploring various folk music styles and playing old-time fiddle music.

Dom Flemons, on the other hand, came to the Black Banjo Gathering from across the country. At the time he performed at the Gathering, he was in his last semester of college in Arizona. A native of the Phoenix area, since his teenage years he had been a regular in the Arizona folk scene.

Rhiannon was thrilled to meet musicians as dynamic and quirky as Justin and Dom. She recognized them as spirits kindred to her own. Musical explorers with intellectual bents, Justin and Dom were as excited as Rhiannon to delve deeper into the African American old-time tradition.

A couple months after the Black Banjo Gathering, Rhiannon flew to Arizona to meet Dom and Sule Greg Wilson, another African American musician from Arizona who had attended the event. The three formed a group, Sankofa Strings, which performed various music styles, including country and classic blues, early jazz, old-time, Caribbean and African music.

Rhiannon enjoyed visiting Arizona, but she had no doubt she'd stay rooted in the Southeast. A few months after the Black Banjo Gathering, she moved back from Richmond to her home state. She moved to Durham, close to Justin Robinson. Also relocating to Durham at the same time was Dom Flemons.

The area was a good fit for these three musicians. A lot of old-time musicians lived there. Recent college graduates made up some of the scene. The rest was made up of veterans steeped in the music for decades, such as Alice Gerrard, editor of the magazine the *Old-Time Herald*.

Thursday evenings in the late summer of 2005, Rhiannon, Justin and Dom met for music sessions at Joe Thompson's house in Mebane. Rhiannon had not been there since 2001, just before his stroke, but she'd heard him at the Black Banjo Gathering and wanted to reconnect.

It took less than a half hour to drive west to Joe's house, and the trip was well worth it. Joe Thompson was back in full musical form.

As we've seen, this iconic African American fiddler was a huge influence on the three young devotees. Joe became their mentor. He was the real deal and a great teacher. He had played his fiddle for square dances seventy years before. He was a window into another era, one that fascinated his three acolytes with a yearning for the past and an eye on the future.

The three younger musicians soaked up Joe's repertoire and techniques. And how fortunate that was. If the three had not met one another at the Black Banjo Gathering and become Joe's protégés, the African American old-time tradition in North Carolina would likely have ended with Joe Thompson.

CREATING THE CAROLINA CHOCOLATE DROPS

That fall of 2005, to keep Joe's old-time music alive, Rhiannon, Justin and Dom formed the Carolina Chocolate Drops. The inspiration for the group's name was a 1930s black string band called the Tennessee Chocolate Drops. The mission of the Carolina Chocolate Drops was to bring the songs Joe Thompson was teaching them out of his private home and into the public arena.

From the onset, the Carolina Chocolate Drops caught people's attention, with standing ovations beginning at their first show. Being a black old-time revival group was a novelty, and there were very few out there. None of the others had their musical talent, youthful good looks and knowledge of musical history. The timing was right. Soon, the Carolina Chocolate Drops were a sensation.

The year 2006 was a very busy one for the group. At the ArtsCenter in Carrboro, they played their first gig, and Rhiannon did a residency. They started playing at town squares and farmers' markets in the Triangle and Greensboro. They began performing in schools around the Piedmont, including at a monthly square dance at the Arts Based Elementary School in Winston-Salem.

They also enjoyed performing at rural schools in North Carolina with a largely African American student body. They felt it was important to signal to rural black children that African Americans aren't just about rap music. The students were trying hard to be urban. Through their show, the Carolina Chocolate Drops sent a message to them: the old-time music black folks played years ago in your town was cool, and without it, today's popular music wouldn't exist.

That same year, the Carolina Chocolate Drops performed at the Shakori Hills Music Festival. There they met Tim Duffy of the Music Maker Relief Foundation, who would go on to manage the group. They also competed at the venerable Mount Airy Fiddlers Convention, where the following year they won the string band category. They started touring around the state, with a few trips beyond.

Rhiannon also studied music in Africa, accepting an invitation from Daniel Jatta, the Gambian musician she'd met at the Black Banjo Gathering.

In 2007, with Rhiannon living back in Greensboro, the Carolina Chocolate Drops released their first CD, *Dona Got a Ramblin' Mind*, named after a song they'd learned from Joe. That same year, they performed in Denzel Washington's film *The Great Debaters* and made their first appearance on *A Prairie Home Companion*. They also started touring the country.

Rhiannon quit her day job and was now a full-time musician, calling contra dances and cobbling together gigs with the Carolina Chocolate Drops.

In 2008, the group became the first African American old-time group to play on the *Grand Ole Opry*. It was a historic event that host Marty Stewart declared a "healing moment." That same year, they released their CD *Heritage* and toured the British Isles and continental Europe.

By 2010, with their busy schedule touring around the United States and Europe, being a Carolina Chocolate Drop had become a full-time job.

In 2010, their album *Genuine Negro Jig* won a Grammy for Best Traditional Folk Album. They appeared on the soundtrack for the film *The Hunger Games*, Amnesty International's tribute to Bob Dylan CD and the Chieftains fiftieth-anniversary CD. That same year, weary of traveling and eager to pursue a graduate degree, Justin Robinson amicably left the group.

The newly configured band thrived with the 2012 release of *Leaving Eden*, which featured the popular song that Rhiannon wrote herself: "Country Girl."

Even with the 2014 departure of Dom Flemons, the group remained strong. Rhiannon attracts top-notch musicians to join the fold, and the Carolina Chocolate Drops continue to wow audiences around the world.

The Carolina Chocolate Drops, *left to right:* Justin Robinson, Rhiannon Giddens and Dom Flemons, Neighborhood Theater, Charlotte, North Carolina, 2006. *Photo by Daniel Coston.*

LEGACY

Rhiannon has a clear view of what she wants her legacy to be: "I want to be remembered for keeping black string band music together and alive."

Rhiannon could be a mainstream star. But what's rare about Rhiannon as a musician is that she's carving out her own niche. The record companies aren't dictating to her. She's paving the way for herself and others to follow.

Instead of looking to Beyoncé for inspiration, Rhiannon looks to Etta Baker (1913–2006), the late, great black blues and old-time musician from Morganton, North Carolina. When Rhiannon met Etta Baker at the Swannanoa Gathering, she fell in love with Baker's amazing music, as well as with Baker herself. Baker reminded her of her grandmother, even down to the clothes she wore. Rhiannon felt an instant connection. Rhiannon's version of Etta Baker's "West End Blues" is a heart-felt tribute to the master.

According to Rhiannon, "I feel honored to be part of the community of North Carolina women of color who play the old songs." She's keeping them alive, giving them a fresh take and bringing them to new audiences. Through Rhiannon, Etta Baker lives on.

As, of course, do Joe Thompson and the thousands of other black old-time musicians before him. Rhiannon, with her virtuoso voice and musicianship, careful research and passion for history, has resurrected a nearly forgotten piece of our state's and country's cultural heritage. We are all the richer as a result.

Happily for North Carolina, Rhiannon is staying connected to her home state. As she told the audience at the 2013 MusicFest 'n Sugar Grove: "The farther I travel, the more I realize I'm so firmly a North Carolinian. My great-grandfather made moonshine. My grandmother made dandelion wine. My dad pulled tobacco."

Rhiannon is getting the attention she deserves, and her star is rising. In January 2015, Rhiannon released her first solo album, *Tomorrow Is My Turn*. The album received great reviews and media coverage. The *New York Times* ran a glowing page-and-a-half article. After Rhiannon sang an African American work song from the album on *The Late Show*, David Letterman ran up to her on stage and cried, "Oh, my God! That was unbelievable!"

Tomorrow Is My Turn pays homage to some of Rhiannon's favorites, including Sister Rosetta Tharpe, Elizabeth Cotten and Odetta. According to Rhiannon, the album "sheds light where it needs to be shed, on the…women of roots music who made such a difference."

Rhiannon Giddens fits right in with the artists she celebrates. She, too, is making a difference. Through her multitude of talents, she's shedding light on America's often forgotten past, resurrecting a repertoire and tradition that has relevance and meaning for all fans of American music.

Rhiannon's Favorite Songs

"Genuine Negro Jig"
"Ruby, Are You Mad at Your Man?"

Essential Carolina Chocolate Drops CDs

Genuine Negro Jig
Heritage
Leaving Eden

Rhiannon Giddens's North Carolina

Contra dances in North Carolina

Highland Games (Linville): In 2004, she won first prize in the Gaelic song competition.

MerleFest (Wilkesboro)

Mount Airy Fiddlers Convention: In 2007, the Carolina Chocolate Drops won first prize.

MusicFest 'n Sugar Grove

Shakori Hills (Pittsboro): This was the first festival she played.

Rhiannon's Websites

CarolinaChocolateDrops.com

RhiannonGiddens.com

GET INVOLVED

I hope that reading the stories in this book has inspired you to dig deeper into North Carolina's old-time and bluegrass music. Here are some ways to get involved:

- Buy CDs of the musicians profiled in this book. Buy their songs on iTunes. Listen to musicians featured on labels like County Sales, Old Blue Records, Old Hat Records and Sugar Hill Records.
- Read magazines such as the *Old-Time Herald*, *Bluegrass Today* and *Bluegrass Unlimited*.
- Visit the Earl Scruggs Center in Shelby, North Carolina; the Old-Time Music Heritage Hall in Mount Airy, North Carolina; and the Blue Ridge Music Center Museum, just across the state line on the Blue Ridge Parkway near Galax, Virginia.
- Go to North Carolina old-time and bluegrass music festivals and events. The Blue Ridge Music Trails of North Carolina and the Blue Ridge National Heritage Area have great websites. For another resource, visit CarolinaMusicWays.org and click on "Explore." Also, check out this book's chapter endings for festivals and events related to the musicians profiled.
- Learn to play banjo, fiddle, guitar, mandolin or upright bass. North Carolina has fantastic music teachers. Contact your local music stores. You can order instructional materials on-line. David Holt has a terrific website. So do others, including Bob Carlin, Brad Leftwich and Wayne Erbsen.

"Parking Lot Jam" by Tracy Bigelow Grisman.

Young musicians at Andy May's Acoustic Kids Showcase, MerleFest, Wilkesboro, North Carolina, 2014 (left) and 2015 (right). *Photos by Jamie Wykl (left) and William Sparklin (right), courtesy of MerleFest.*

I'm happy to hear from readers at the following e-mail address: LizCarlsonBooks@gmail.com.

Whatever path you take to explore North Carolina's old-time and bluegrass treasures, may the music masters you've read about in this book be with you in spirit.

Enjoy your adventure.

My musical adventure began with my dad years ago. Dad loved music, and he shared that passion with me. When a song moves me, I think of Dad.

May the great old-time and bluegrass music of North Carolina bring you happy thoughts of those you love. May it make your heart sing.

SELECTED BIBLIOGRAPHY

I used many sources in researching and writing this book. Not all are included here, but I have listed the sources that I used the most.

CHAPTER I

Quotations in this chapter with no source cited are from Kinney Rorrer's biography, *Rambling Blues: The Life & Songs of Charlie Poole*. When I interviewed Rorrer, he shared with me new information he had learned about Charlie Poole since he wrote his book.

Ancestry.com. [To access public records, I used this resource for all chapters in this book.]

Carlin, Bob. *String Bands in the North Carolina Piedmont*. Jefferson, NC: McFarland & Company, Inc., 2004. [This book was also helpful for the Tommy Jarrell and Joe Thompson chapters.]

Carlin, Richard. *Country Music: A Biographical Dictionary*. New York: Routledge, 2003.

Fleck, Béla, Kinney Rorrer, Hank Sapoznick and Tony Trischka. "Charlie Poole: You Ain't Talkin' to Me." Interview by Laura Cantrell. PRX audio, May 5, 2005. https://beta.prx.org/stories/4499.

Goehl, George, Jocelyn Neal (moderator), Kinney Rorrer and Hank Sapoznick. *Dynamic Legacies: Charlie Poole Conference, April 8, 2005*. Southern Folklife Collection, Wilson Library, University of North Carolina at Chapel Hill. Compact disc FS7982.

Huber, Patrick. *Linthead Stomp: The Creation of Country Music in the Piedmont South*. Chapel Hill: University of North Carolina, 2008.

Knauff, Gail (director, Haw River Historical Association Museum). Interview with the author, July 12, 2014.

Mazor, Barry. "Charlie Poole's Outlaw Country: 80 Years Old—and Hot." *Wall Street Journal*, last updated July 27, 2005. http://www.wsj.com/news/articles/SB112241618930996641.

Rorrer, Kinney (Charlie Poole biographer and grandnephew of Charlie Poole and Posey Rorer). Interview with the author, July 29, 2014.

————. *Rambling Blues: The Life & Songs of Charlie Poole*. Danville, VA: McCain, 1982.

Rubin, Mark. "Charlie Poole: The Man at Country Music's Roots." *Sing Out!* 49, no. 3 (Fall 2005): 18–24.

Sapoznick, Hank. *You Ain't Talkin' to Me: Charlie Poole and the Roots of Country Music*. Sony, 2005. Compact disc box set liner notes.

Wainwright, Loudon, III. *High Wide and Handsome: The Charlie Poole Project*. Project booklet. 2009. http://www.thecharliepooleproject.com/CharlieBook-Web.pdf.

Whatley, L. McKay (president, Randolph Heritage Conservancy). Interview with the author, July 15, 2014.

————. "Manly Reese." "Notes on the History of Randolph County, NC" (blog). September 15, 2009. https://randolphhistory.wordpress.com/2009/09/15/manly-reece.

————. "More on Charlie Poole and Daner Johnson." "Notes on the History of Randolph County, NC" (blog). July 15, 2014. https://randolphhistory.wordpress.com/tag/millboro.

CHAPTER 2

Alden, Ray G. "Music From Round Peak." *Sing Out!* 21, no. 6 (November–December 1972): 1–11.

————. "Tommy Jarrell and Fred Cockerham: North Carolina Fiddle and Fretless Banjo." *Tommy and Fred: Best Fiddle-Banjo Duets*. County Records, 1994. Compact disc liner notes reprinted with permission of the author. http://www.mustrad.org.uk/articles/jarrell.htm.

Brown, Paul (musician, journalist, producer). Interview with the author, September 25, 2014.

————. "Remembrances—The Connector: Ray Alden (July 2, 1942–September 19, 2009)." *Old-Time Herald* 12, no. 2 (n.d.). http://www.oldtimeherald.org/archive/back_issues/volume-12/12-2/alden.html.

Donleavy, Kevin. *Strings of Life: Conversations with Old-Time Musicians from Virginia and North Carolina*. Blacksburg, VA: Pocahontas Press, 2004.

Faurot, Charles. "Historic Recordings Tell Clawhammer Banjo History." Audio story by Paul Brown. *All Things Considered*, NPR, March 21, 2006. http://www.npr.org/templates/story/story.php?storyId=5293105.

Jabbour, Alan (founder of the American Folklife Center in the Library of Congress). Interview with the author, October 21, 2014.

King, Christopher (production coordinator at County Records). Discussion with the author, September 26, 2014.

Leftwich, Brad. *Old-Time Fiddle Round Peak Style: History, Tips, Techniques*. Pacific, MO: Mel Bay Publications, 2011.

Lyons, Thomas Reavis. "Old-Time Fiddlers Hall of Fame: Thomas Jefferson Jarrell." Old-Time Music Home Page. http://www.oldtimemusic.com/FHOFJarrell.html.

McGee, Marty. *Traditional Musicians of the Central Blue Ridge: Old Time, Early Country, Folk and Bluegrass Label Recording Artists with Discographies.* Jefferson, NC: McFarland, 1999.

Mylet, Tom. "Charles Faurot." *Banjo Newsletter,* July 2013. https://banjonews. com/2013-07/charles_faurot_old_time_recorder.html.

Neithammer, Nancy Dols. "Tommy Jarrell's Family Stories 1830-1925, Part 1." *Old Time Herald* 3, no. 1 (August–October 1991). http://archive.fiddlesessions.com/ oct07/Neithammer.html.

Ruchala, James Randolph. "Making Round Peak Music: History, Revitalization, and Community." PhD diss., Brown University, 2011. https://repository.library. brown.edu/studio/item/bdr:11260.

Snyder, Amy (curator, Mount Airy Museum of Regional History). Discussion with the author, September 26, 2014.

Sprout Wings and Fly. Directed by Les Blank, Cecilia Conway, Alice Gerrard and Maureen Gosling. 1983. El Cerrito, CA: Flower Films, 2012. DVD.

Thompson, Evelyn (president of the African American Historical and Genealogical Society of Surry County). Discussion with the author, September 28, 2014.

White, Wallace. "Our Far-Flung Correspondents: Fiddling." *New Yorker,* July 20, 1987, 74–88.

CHAPTER 3

Carlin, Bob (old-time musician and historian). Interview with the author, April 29, 2015.

Chapman, Iris Thompson (professor, documentarian, Joe Thompson's second cousin). Interview with the author, May 21, 2015.

Chapman, Iris Thompson, Bob Carlin, Glenn Hinson and Wayne Martin. "The Legacy of Joe Thompson." Interview by Frank Stasio. *The State of Things.* WUNC Radio. April 5, 2012. http://wunc.org/post/legacy-joe-thompson.

Conway, Cecilia. *African Banjo Echoes in Appalachia: A Study of Folk Traditions.* Knoxville: University of Tennessee Press, 1995.

Flemons, Dom. "Carolina Chocolate Drops Mentor, Joe Thompson, Passes Away." *Music Maker Relief Foundation Newsletter,* "B'man's Blues Report" (blog), February 23, 2012. http://www.bmansbluesreport.com/2012/02/carolina-chocolate-drops-mentor-joe.html.

Ivey, Dellaphine (Joe Thompson's niece). Interview with the author, May 26, 2015.

Killian, Joe. "Joe Thompson Documentary Showcases Fiddler." *Greensboro News & Record,* October 7, 2004. http://www.news-record.com/joe-thompson-documentary-showcases-fiddler/article_006980d5-8fd5-5c4c-9ce6-9d348077155c.html.

Lornell, Kip (professor, ethnomusicologist). Interview with the author, May 29, 2015.

Martin, Douglas. "Joe Thompson Dies at 93; Helped Preserve the Black String Band." *New York Times,* March 1, 2012. http://www.nytimes.com/2012/03/02/ arts/music/joe-thompson-dies-at-93-fiddler-of-string-band-legacy.html.

Menconi, David. "North Carolina Folk Musician Dies at 93." *Charlotte Observer,* February 22, 2012. http://mudcat.org/thread.cfm?threadid=143462.

Ritchie, Fiona, and Doug Orr. *Wayfaring Strangers: The Musical Voyage from Scotland and Ulster to Appalachia.* Chapel Hill: University of North Carolina Press, 2014.

Romtvedt, David. "Octogenarian Fiddler Joe Thompson is a Master of the Frolic Tradition." *All Things Strings*, December 2007. http://www.allthingsstrings. com/layout/set/print/News/Interviews-Profiles/Octogenarian-Fiddler-Joe-Thompson-Is-a-Master-of-the-Frolic-Tradition.

Rowe, Jerri. "A Man of Tradition: Joe Thompson, the Nation's Only Living Traditional Fiddle Player Who Is African American, Keeps Black History Alive through His Music." *Greensboro News & Record*, January 7, 1999. http://www. greensboro.com/a-man-of-tradition-joe-thompson-the-nation-s-only/article_ e0194177-4171-57aa-8b5f-e3a54c70fc4d.html.

Steel Drivin' Man: The Life and Times of Joe Thompson. Directed and produced by Iris Thompson Chapman. 2004. DVD.

Thompson, Joe. "A Visit with Joe Thompson." Interview by Eli Smith. *Down Home Radio Show* podcast, October 6, 2010. http://www.downhomeradioshow. com/2010/10/a-visit-with-joe-thompson.

Thompson, Joe, Dom Flemons, Rhiannon Giddens and Justin Robinson. "Lessons from the Master." Interview by Dick Gordon. *The Story.* WUNC Radio, March 21, 2007. http://www.thestory.org/stories/2007-03/lessons-master.

Wells, Paul F. "Fiddling as an Avenue of Black-White Musical Interchange." *Black Music Research Journal* 23, nos. 1–2 (March 22, 2003): 135.

CHAPTER 4

Cantwell, Robert. *Bluegrass Breakdown: The Making of the Old Southern Sound.* New York: Da Capo, 1992.

Cantwell, Robert, T. Michael Coleman, Jim Collier, David Holt, George Holt, Barry Poss and Joe Wilson. "Doc Watson Symposium: Panel II—The Folk Revival and Beyond." North Carolina Museum of Art, June 30, 2012. YouTube video, 1:09, posted July 9, 2012. https://www.youtube.com/watch?v=zl28sEFd-tc.

Coleman, T. Michael, Jim Collier, David Holt, George Holt, Wayne Henderson, Jeff Little, Wayne Martin and Bryan Sutton. "Doc Watson Symposium: Panel III—The Music." North Carolina Museum of Art, June 30, 2012. YouTube video, 1:22, posted July 9, 2012. https://www.youtube.com/watch?v=hMg6EnEC0c8.

Gerrard, Phillip. "Doc." *Our State*, special ed., *100 North Carolina Icons*, July 2012, 114–24.

Grimes, Williams. "Doc Watson, Blind Guitar Wizard Who Influenced Millions, Dies at 89." *New York Times*, May 29, 2012. http://www.nytimes.com/2012/05/30/ arts/music/doc-watson-folk-musician-dies-at-89.html.

Gustavson, Kent. *Blind but Now I See: The Biography of Music Legend Doc Watson.* New York: Blooming Twig Books, 2010.

Holt, David. "Conversations with Doc Watson." *Folkways*, WUNC-TV, December 1, 2010. http://video.unctv.org/video/1716852757.

Holt, David, and Doc Watson. *Doc Watson and David Holt: Legacy.* Fairview, NC: High Windy Audio, 2002. Compact disc set and booklet.

Holt, David, George Holt, Wayne Martin, David Watson, Kermit Watson and Joe Wilson. "Doc Watson Symposium: Panel I—Early Influences and the Beginning." North Carolina Museum of Art, June 30, 2012. YouTube video, 1:27, posted July 9, 2012. https://www.youtube.com/watch?v=4maUvlRlkbM.

Kaufman, Steve. *The Legacy of Doc Watson*. Pacific, MO: Mel Bay, 1999.

Santelli, Robert, Holly George-Warren and Jim Brown. *American Roots Music*. New York: H.N. Abrams, 2001.

"Three Days with Doc." Narrated by A.L. Lloyd. Omnibus USA. British Broadcasting Corporation, 1976. YouTube video, 0:34, posted July 12, 2002. https://www.youtube.com/watch?v=i5mZlriOogU.

Watson, David, Kermit Watson and David Holt (Doc Watson's brother, nephew and musical partner, respectively). Interview with the author, December 7, 2013.

Watson, Doc. "Fresh Air Remembers Traditional Music Legend Doc Watson." Interview by Terry Gross. *Fresh Air*. WBUR Radio, May 29, 2012. Original interview, March 24, 1988. http://www.wbur.org/npr/153704132/fresh-air-remembers-traditional-music-legend-doc-watson.

Watson, Nancy. *Milestones: Legends of the Doc Watson Clan*. Johnson City, TN: Open Records, 2013. Book and compact disc set.

CHAPTER 5

Borchelt, Don. "Shade Tree Picking." Banj'r website. 2008. http://www.banjr.com/shade%20tree%20picking.htm.

Carlin, Bob. "Earl and the 3-Finger Style." *Banjo Newsletter*, May 2012. https://banjonews.com/2012-05/earl_and_3-finger_style.html.

————. "Roots of Earl and Snuffy." Remember Cliffside website of the Cliffside Historical Society. Article originally appeared in *Bluegrass Unlimited*, May 2009. http://remembercliffside.com/history/the_county/hammett/hammett.html.

Cooper, Peter. "Earl Scruggs, Country Music Hall of Famer and Bluegrass Innovator, Dies at 88." "The Tennessean" (blog), March 28, 2012. http://blogs.tennessean.com/tunein/2012/03/28/earl-scruggs-country-music-hall-of-famer-dies-at-age-88.

Dawidoff, Nicholas. *In the Country of Country: A Journey to the Roots of American Music*. New York: Vintage Books, 1998.

Depriest, Joe. "Scruggs Travels Hard Road to Regain Spirit; N.C. Bluegrass Great Renews Fervor for Banjo after Years of Pain." *Charlotte Observer*, August 26, 2001.

Earl Scruggs Center, Shelby, NC. Notes taken by the author on a tour of the museum, January 17, 2015.

Earl Scruggs Family and Friends. Directed by David Hoffman. 1972. Los Angeles: Cleopatra, 2006. DVD.

Erbsen, Wayne. "Wiley & Zeke Morris, the Morris Brothers." Native Ground Books & Music website. http://nativeground.com/wiley-a-zeke-morris-the-morris-brothers-by-wayne-erbsen.

Gitlin, Ira. "Earl Scruggs: An End and a Beginning (Or What Does a Banjo Player Have in Common with Homer and Sir Isaac Newton?" BluegrassSpecial.com. April

2012. http://www.thebluegrassspecial.com/archive/2012/april2012/earl-scruggs-ira-gitlin.html.

Heaton, C.P. "The 5-String Banjo in North Carolina." Native Ground Books & Music website. http://nativeground.com/the-5-string-banjo-in-north-carolina-by-cp-heaton.

Holt, George. "Recorded in Charlotte." History South website, based on the booklet by George Holt, *The Charlotte Country Music Story*, 1985. http://www.historysouth.org/recordedinclt.

Malone, Bill C. *Country Music, U.S.A.* Rev. ed. Austin: University of Texas Press, 1985.

Martin, Steve. "The Master from Flint Hill: Earl Scruggs." *New Yorker*, January 13, 2012. http://www.newyorker.com/culture/culture-desk/the-master-from-flint-hill-earl-scruggs.

Mills, Jim (bluegrass musician and historian). Interview with the author, April 21, 2015.

Rosenberg, Neil V. *Bluegrass: A History*. Urbana: University of Illinois Press, 1993.

Scruggs, Earl. *Earl Scruggs and the 5-String Banjo*. Rev. and enhanced ed. Milwaukee, WI: Hal Leonard, 2005.

————. "Earl Scruggs: The 2003 Fresh Air Interview." Interview by Terry Gross. *Fresh Air*, WBUR Radio, March 29, 2012. Original interview, 2003. http://www.npr.org/2012/03/30/149612506/earl-scruggs-the-2003-fresh-air-interview.

Scruggs, Earl, and John Hartford. "The Story of 'Foggy Mountain Breakdown.'" Audio story by Paul Brown. *Weekend Edition Saturday*, NPR, April 1, 2000. http://www.npr.org/2000/04/01/1072355/npr-100-earl-scruggs.

Trischka, Tony. "DeWitt 'Snuffy' Jenkins." *Bluegrass Unlimited*, October 1977, 20–21. http://www.folkstreams.net/principal,491.

Trischka, Tony, and Béla Fleck. "Earl Scruggs: Interview by Tony Trischka and Béla Fleck." *Banjo Newsletter*, May 2012. https://banjonews.com/2012-05/interview_with_earl_scruggs_(2006).html.

Chapter 6

Quotations attributed to David Holt in this chapter are from my interview with him, listed below.

DavidHolt.com. "Articles and Interviews." http://www.davidholt.com/about/articles-and-interview.

Holt, David. "David Holt's State of Music." Audio interview by Frank Stasio and Hady Mawajdeh. *The State of Things*, WUNC Radio, January 12, 2015. http://wunc.org/post/david-holts-state-music-1.

————. "David Holt: The Joyful Tradition of Mountain Music." *TED Talk*, March 2004. https://www.ted.com/talks/david_holt_plays_mountain_music.

————. Interview with the author for this chapter, September 25, 2014.

Holt, David, Will McIntyre and Deni McIntyre. *David Holt's State of Music*, UNC-TV special. January 29, 2015.

Keding, Dan. "David Holt: Holding on to Treasures." *Sing Out!* 41, no. 1 (May 1, 1996).

Prather, Jack J. *Twelve Notables in Western North Carolina*. Hendersonville, NC: Future Now Publishing, 2012.

Rifkin, Carol. "Doc Watson and David Holt." *Acoustic Guitar* 22, no. 6 (December 2011): 62–66.

CHAPTER 7

Unless otherwise indicated in this chapter, any quotations attributed to Rhiannon Giddens are from my interview with her, listed below.

Flemons, Dom (musician, co-founder, Carolina Chocolate Drops). Interview with the author, September 12, 2013.

Giddens, Rhiannon. Interview with the author, September 11, 2013.

———. "Rhiannon Giddens." Audio story by Brian Bahouth, PRX Radio, posted April 2013. http://www.prx.org/pieces/96280-rhiannon-giddens.

Giddens, Rhiannon, and Dom Flemons. "Carolina Chocolate Drops: Hooked on Old-Time Sounds." Interview by Scott Simon. *Weekend Edition Saturday*, NPR, March 9, 2012. http://www.npr.org/2012/03/10/148300894/carolina-chocolate-drops-hooked-on-old-time-sounds.

Giddens, Rhiannon, Dom Flemons and Justin Robinson. "Carolina Chocolate Drops on World Café." Interview by David Dye. *World Café*, WXPN Radio, June 24, 2010. http://www.npr.org/templates/story/story.php?storyId=122620195.

———. "Carolina Chocolate Drops: Tradition from Jug to Kazoo." Interview by Terry Gross. *Fresh Air*, WBUR Radio, March 1, 2010. http://www.npr.org/2010/03/01/123968480/carolina-chocolate-drops-tradition-from-jug-to-kazoo.

Pareles, Jon. "A Solo Spotlight for a Powerful Voice." *New York Times*, January 25, 2015. http://www.nytimes.com/2015/01/25/arts/music/a-solo-spotlight-for-a-powerful-voice.html.

Silcox-Jarrett, Diane. "The Origin of Carolina Chocolate Drops." *Our State*, January 1, 2010. http://www.ourstate.com/carolina-chocolate-drops.

Wilcock, Don. "The Interview of the Week; Rhiannon Giddens of the Carolina Chocolate Drops." The Alternate Root. http://thealternateroot.com/index.php?option=com_content&view=article&id=1002:interview-with-rhiannon-giddens&catid=208&Itemid=268.

INDEX

ABOUT THE AUTHOR

Elizabeth A. Carlson is the founder and education director of Carolina Music Ways, a nonprofit group that educates North Carolina schoolchildren about their state's diverse musical heritage. She holds degrees in English and American studies from Princeton University and in language and literacy from the Harvard Graduate School of Education. She lives with her husband in Winston-Salem, North Carolina.

Photo by Katie Dickson Photography, 2015.